From

Now

to

Eternity

From

Now

to

Eternity

From Now to Eternity

*Sermons from the
Book of Revelation
Presenting the Future
History of the World*

Nathan M. Meyer

BMH Books

Winona Lake, Indiana 46590

DEDICATION

This book is dedicated to the memory of my mother, who prayed before I was born that her "firstborn son might be a preacher."

Her prayer was answered thirty years later, and she lived to hear these messages as they were delivered. But she went to heaven before they were put into print.

First Printing, December 1976
Second Printing, April 1981
Third Printing, March 1984

Cover design and art: Tim Kennedy

ISBN: 0-88469-035-0

COPYRIGHT 1976
BMH BOOKS
WINONA LAKE, INDIANA

Printed in U.S.A.

Introduction

These messages were first delivered a number of years ago while the author was pastor of the Grace Brethren Church in Leesburg, Indiana.

The writer has been devoting his time to Bible prophecy conferences since 1959. He has delivered these messages to interested audiences on several continents from Kenya, East Africa; to Kenai, Alaska, involving hundreds of churches, large and small. Various Bible conferences such as the American and Canadian Keswick have received them with enthusiasm. They have also been broadcast from coast to coast over the air.

The Lord has used them to bring hundreds of precious but lost souls to a saving knowledge of Jesus Christ. Thousands of individuals have testified to the truth of Revelation 1:3:

> Blessed is he that readeth and they that hear the words of this prophecy . . . .

So many books have been written about the Book of Revelation that the author hesitated to add another one. But with increasing persistence during the last ten years, listeners, in increasing numbers, have been pressing this preacher to "put those messages in print."

Thousands of tape recordings have been made in many places from Africa to Hawaii. Praise the Lord for tape recorders! But now at last they are "written in a book" for all who wish to read. It is the author's sincere and devout prayer that the Lord will supernaturally compensate for all human errors, deficiencies, and discrepancies.

May many mixed-up mortals, young and old, schooled and unschooled, who have never found the answers to the great questions of life, find them in this book. *FROM NOW TO ETERNITY* is the *story of the future history of the world.* It is inseparably tied up with the Biblical account of how God is going to reveal His Son to the whole universe in mighty power.

May all those who have never learned to love that One who is "altogether lovely" see Him in these pages so they will come to love Him, too. And may the divinely revealed knowledge of things to come help the reader to live in the present so he can eagerly welcome the future.

Table of Contents

Part One

The Things Which
Thou Hast Seen

I

The Person
of Christ

INTRODUCTION

It's a fascinating story! Everybody ought to know it! It is the most magnificent scene ever displayed to earthlings. And it comes to us through the eyes and pen of John, the beloved disciple. Yet very few people know anything about it.

We are beginning our study of the phenomenal book called: The Revelation of Jesus Christ. Please open your Bible to the very last book.

In verses 1-3 and also verse 19 we will deal with the introduction and in the rest of the chapter we will deal with a portrait of Christ. This is the essence of the first chapter. Now look at the very first verse of the first chapter. Here we have the

TITLE AND THEME:
THE REVELATION OF JESUS CHRIST

The word "Revelation" shouldn't frighten you. It means to reveal or to publicly present to open view.

So here we have the story of how God the Father is going to publicly present to the universe, in mighty power, His lovely Son. It is the magnificent story of the future history of the world from John's day (about A.D. 100) on into the eternal ages. There is absolutely no other book in the world like it.

APOCALYPSE

This book was first written in Greek and the Greek word for Revelation is Apocalypse. Therefore, you need not be surprised to find (as in the Catholic Bible) that this book is called: The Apocalypse. And who has not heard of the four horsemen of the Apocalypse? Yet almost nobody knows who they are. We read about them in chapter 6, and we shall see how John explains them when we reach that point.

THE DIVINE AUTHOR

Now notice another thing we are told in verse 1: God is the divine author. It says, ". . . which God gave. . . ."

THE RECIPIENTS

". . . to show unto his servants. . . ." The book was written to

God's children. It is really a love-letter from God to the believers, written in language which only they can understand, to give them special information that God wants them to know. The believers are the recipients of this message.

THE CONTENT — PROPHECY

Now notice the phrase: ". . . things which must shortly come to pass. . . ." That's future history; that's predictive prophecy! This is most important. Do not miss it! We are studying a *book of prophecy*. Keep that in mind all the way through.

As you read on, you discover that the message was delivered by an angel and recorded by John as an eyewitness. So what we have here is an eyewitness account of what John saw. Who in absence can argue with such a witness who was present and saw?

SPECIAL BLESSING GUARANTEED

Take a look at the third verse, please. This is unusual in the Bible. While you receive a blessing in the study of any portion of the Word, it is unique for the Bible to say that you get a special blessing from studying a special part, yet that is exactly what we have in verse 3:

> Blessed is he that *readeth*, and they that *hear* the words of this prophecy, and *keep* those things which are written therein: for the time is at hand.

You have a guarantee in writing by a God that cannot lie that if you study this book and listen to its exposition, and then go out to put into practice that which you have learned, God will bless you. More than that, it will be a special blessing. Here is your guarantee. And I have never yet seen it fail.

If this is true then why is this book so neglected and why do so few ever really study it? The reason—well, this is the book that tells how the devil will finally be thrown into the lake of eternal fire. It is the account of how Lucifer is going to meet his end, and so he hates this book with a vengeance, probably more than any other book in the Bible. Therefore, he has worked overtime, so to speak, trying to get preachers and church members to stay out of this book, and unfortunately, he has succeeded very well.

I'm sorry that is true, but it is. So I hope you will not let Satan influence you with the argument that this book is too difficult for anybody to understand and that you really ought to stay out of it because it is full of deep, dark symbols. This is the argument that is used. But I can assure you that if you will bring your Bible and be in your place each night as we go through the book, and if you are really searching for the truth and will open your heart to the Holy Spirit, He will pour out tremendous blessings upon you. And He will cause you to praise the Lord as you watch His glory and power unfold. It cannot be otherwise, because God guarantees it.

I want to go now to verse 19 to show you the specific instructions Jesus gave John concerning the

OUTLINE FOR THIS BOOK

This is extremely important. This verse causes me to be very narrow-minded and dogmatic. It says: "Write the things which thou hast seen [Part I], and the things which are [Part II], and the things which shall be hereafter [Part III]." The Lord Jesus Himself tells John to write a book which shall be divided into three parts: (1) the things you have just seen. That must be chapter 1, because it is past tense and it is at the end of chapter 1. Then, (2) the things that are now. As we shall see, that covers chapters 2 and 3. And then, (3) the things which will be in the future. That is chapter 4 and following to the end of the book. That must be true because the very first verse of chapter 4 ends with this line: ". . . Come up hither, and I will shew thee *things which must be hereafter.*" This is Jesus' own outline and there is no room for argument. Any attempt to fit the book, beginning with chapter 4, into past history is contrary to Jesus' outline.

IT IS A BOOK OF PROPHECY! AND FROM CHAPTER FOUR ON, IT IS FUTURE FROM OUR POINT IN TIME.

ON THE ISLE OF PATMOS

Our story begins with John, as an aged man and pastor of the church in Ephesus, banished from his people to the barren, desolate, rocky island of Patmos. Ephesus was located on what is today the coast of Turkey. There isn't much left of Ephesus but a few ruins. As a matter of fact, quite a few ruins. In recent years they have been unearthing the ancient city of Ephesus, and now one can walk the streets of Ephesus where the apostle Paul walked. One can sit in the stadium where 25,000 Ephesians shouted "Great is Diana of the Ephesians." One can look down to the harbor and see where the apostle Paul landed and one can see the stones which form the main street where he walked coming up from the habor to the city—all of these have just recently been excavated. You can even walk into the ruins of some of the "houses of love" as they were called in the wicked, immoral, licentious city of Ephesus.

Ephesus is today a city of ruins. But in the first century, John was the pastor of a fine church in that city. Then the authorities came and took away the pastor of this church, the aged, beloved disciple John. They banished him as I said, to the lonely, desolate island of Patmos in the Aegean Sea, not far off the coast of what today is known as Turkey.

DRAMA OF FUTURE PORTRAYED

It was Sunday morning and John must have been deep in meditation and prayer, not at all expecting what was about to happen. Suddenly God opened the heavens, and in the power of the Holy Spirit let John see the whole panorama of history yet to be. The whole drama of the *future history of the world* from his day on into the eternal ages was portrayed before his eyes. Think of that! John was an eyewitness. And then the Holy Spirit guarded and guided John's pen so that he wrote exactly what God wanted written. The result is the book called "The Revelation of Jesus Christ."

It is therefore most appropriate that John, in the very first chapter of his book, should show us a picture of Christ as he saw Him and as He would appear today if we could see Him in person in all His power and glory. The first three verses gave us the introduction, and now we have a picture dealing first of all with

THE ATTRIBUTES AND ACTIVITIES OF CHRIST

Beginning with verse 4 let us notice especially what Christ is and what He does:

John to the seven churches which are in Asia: Grace be unto you, and peace. . . .

Two special gifts that come from God alone and only to those who love Him—grace and peace. Christ is the giver of grace and peace. And so John says:

. . . from him which is, and which was, and which is to come. . . .

We have here three verb phrases suggesting past, present and future—indicating the eternity of the Godhead. Christ is eternal; He always was, is now, and always will be. We will meet these phrases again in verse 8 and in a number of future chapters.

. . . and from the seven Spirits which are before his throne.

You know there is only one Holy Spirit, but the reference here, I am sure, is to seven special spiritual beings or seven angels, and we will meet these seven angels again from time to time. I will have more to say about them when next we see them in chapters 4 and 5.

And from Jesus Christ, who is the faithful witness, and the first begotten of the dead, and the prince of the kings of the earth. Unto him that loved us, and washed us from our sins in his own blood, and hath made us . . . .

This is one of my favorite passages of the entire Bible. Three things that Christ has done for us: He *loved us* so much that He left the glories of the Father's house and came to earth below and allowed Himself to be smitten, to be beaten, to be spit upon, to be mocked, and to be crucified. He loved us with an everlasting love.

More than that! He *washed us*. We needed it. We were sinners. We are all sinners by nature and sinners by choice. Paul wrote in Romans 3:23: "For all have sinned, and come short of the glory of God." And in chapter 3, verse 10: "There is none righteous, no, not one." The Lord washed us from our sins. He cleansed every guilty stain and washed us whiter than snow. He loved us and He washed us from our sins in His own blood. This is the reason why God can look at us, worms of the dust, sinners by birth and sinners by choice, and call us perfect—all because we have been washed in the blood of the Lamb.

This is one of the marvels of God's revealed truth. All of us know that none of us is perfect, yet God says we are. He declares us to be saints. Imagine that! Saints are not made by a declaration of the papacy or of some earthly church. Saints are made as God declares mortals to be saints, and He declares all those who accept Christ as Saviour to be saints.

There is something very interesting in this regard in the Book of Corinthians. Incidentally, that is one church where I would never have wanted to be pastor; they had too many troubles. They were loaded with problems pertaining to all kinds of sins and carnalities. In effect, Paul said to them: "I would like to write to you as if you were mature Christians, but you aren't. You are yet carnal. I would like to feed you some spiritual meat, but you couldn't take it; you would choke on it. So I have to keep you on the bottle. You are spiritual babies." He tells them, "Ye are yet carnal; I would like to write to you as if you were spiritual. But you are not spiritual; you are carnal." I am paraphrasing, of course. Earlier, in his letter he calls them all saints. That is a marvelous thing. He tells them how carnal they are, and yet God calls them saints. See I Corinthians 1:2 and 6:2.

The late Dr. Alva J. McClain was the greatest theologian I ever knew and the greatest teacher I ever had. Because of his illness and frailty he never became well known in the world. But he was the founding president of the Grace Theological Seminary, and those who enjoy my ministry owe a debt to Dr. McClain. In one of his theology classes he told us this story.

He said when he was a pastor he was reprimanding—I guess

that is the proper word—one of his parishioners because of a life that was not too exemplary, and this man (a professing believer) said to his pastor: "Well, Pastor, I don't claim to be a saint."

To this Dr. McClain replied: "But God says you are one, and it is high time you should start living like one."

You see, when we accept Jesus Christ as Saviour, we do not become perfect in our own condition, but we become perfect in position. And it should be our effort to try, in the power of the Holy Spirit, to grow in holiness toward that which is our position in Christ. We can never entirely reach a state of perfect and complete sanctification here below. The Bible speaks of three aspects of sanctification: We are sanctified now in the present. We have been sanctified in the past. And we shall be sanctified in the future. Sanctification will not be complete until we stand in His presence. He will complete it. Nevertheless, in the meantime, we strive toward that point. Yet it is amazing that we who are sinners should be declared to be saints. And this is all possible because He washed us from our sins in His own blood.

And then there is a great climax in this trinity of ideas here in verses 5 and 6. He loved us, He washed us, and He *made us*. It says He hath made us kings and priests. Have you ever secretly wished that you were a prince or a princess? Have you ladies ever envied Princess Grace of Monaco? Or you men, have you wished you had been born a prince? I have good news for you. No earthly monarch can hold a candle to what we are talking about here. Those who have been born into the family of God through faith in Jesus Christ have royal blood in their veins, and are kings and priests of God—members of the royal household of heaven. This exceeds anything you could dream about as far as earthly monarchs are concerned. So don't hang your head when you walk down the street. Lift up your head and sing. You are a prince—you are a king!

We'll sing about it in heaven as we shall see in chapter 5. Meanwhile, let's rejoice and give Christ all the praise because of what He has done.

He hath made us kings and priests unto God and his Father; to him be glory and dominion for ever and ever. Amen.

To Him! To Christ! The whole book is about Christ, and we are going to honor Him. Everything is centered in Him. He deserves all the glory. So it says, "To Him be glory and dominion." How long? "For ever and ever." After a statement like that, what else can we say but—go ahead and say it, Amen! That means: So be it, Lord. So be it, Lord!

THE KEY VERSE

Now in verse 7 we have a summary of the whole Book of Revelation. One might call it the key verse. Remember the title and theme of this book: The Revelation of Jesus Christ. So this verse says:

> Behold, he cometh with clouds; and every eye shall see him, and they also which pierced him: and all kindreds of the earth shall wail because of him. Even so, Amen.

This is not speaking of the rapture. At the rapture, only those for whom He is coming will see Him. On the road to Damascus, Paul saw the Lord, but those who were with Paul did not see Him. When Christ ascended, only His close friends and followers who were gathered around Him on the top of the Mount of Olives saw Him go up. The angel said: "This same Jesus . . . shall so come in like manner as ye have seen him go." Those who are saved will see Him when He comes in the air and will rise to meet Him (cf. I Thess. 4:16). The rest of the world, I am sure, will not see Him at that time.

UNIVERSAL ACCLAMATION

But seven years later, when He comes back *with* the saints, then every eye shall see Him, every knee shall bow, and every tongue shall confess that Jesus Christ is Lord. It won't do them any good at that point because it will be too late, but they will be forced to recognize Him. They will be forced to see Him. They will be forced to acknowledge that He is the omnipotent God.

> Behold, he cometh with clouds; and every eye shall see him, and they also which pierced him: and all the kindreds of the earth shall

wail because of him. Even so, Amen. I am Alpha and Omega, the beginning and the ending, saith the Lord, which is, and which was, and which is to come, the Almighty (Rev. 1:7-8).

"They also which pierced him" refers, of course, to the Jews who ordered His crucifixion. But don't blame them: We all were responsible for His death. He died for *our* sins.

In chapter 7 we shall see that God seals 144,000 of His chosen earthly people so that they can't be destroyed by the plagues of the Tribulation period. Thus, they are supernaturally preserved so they will be alive when Messiah comes in the clouds—and they will recognize Him. Of them Paul says (Rom. 11:26), "And so all Israel shall be saved . . . ."

Speaking of the same group Jesus says, "But he that shall endure unto the end [that is, of the Tribulation period], the same shall be saved." And Zechariah the prophet says of the same group ". . . and they shall look upon me whom they have pierced, and they shall mourn for him, as one mourneth for his only son . . ." (Zech. 12:10).

In verses 9 and 10 John says:

I John, who also am your brother, and companion in tribulation, and in the kingdom and patience of Jesus Christ, was in the isle that is called Patmos, for the word of God, and for the testimony of Jesus Christ.

I was in the Spirit on the Lord's day, and heard behind me a great voice, as of a trumpet.

God loves to have the trumpet sound, and you will find the trumpet associated with God's voice again and again in the Bible.

WRITE IT IN A BOOK

Verse 11:

Saying, I am Alpha and Omega, the first and the last: and, What thou seest, write in a book, and send it unto the seven churches which are in Asia. . . .

John must have thought, "Which seven do you mean? There are more than seven churches in that territory." But of course he doesn't interrupt, and the Lord who is speaking here proceeds to give John His instructions and to spell it out: "Unto

Ephesus."

"Ah, yes, my church," John must have thought. "There my people are this morning without a pastor. I was just praying for them."

"Unto Ephesus," he is told, and "unto Smyrna." That's up the coast a short distance. And "unto Pergamus, and unto Thyatira, and unto Sardis, and unto Philadelphia, and unto Laodicea." And there they are—all seven.

But why seven? God seems to use numbers symbolically and significantly. The number seven denotes the whole. Seven days make the whole week. As we shall see in our next message, we have seven historic churches described in a special sequence, all of which is also prophetic, describing seven periods of church history.

John uses the number seven more than fifty times in the Book of Revelation.

SEVEN GOLDEN CANDLESTICKS

Now let us look at verse 12:

> And I turned to see the voice that spake with me. And being turned, I saw seven golden candlesticks.

Later on, in verse 20, he tells us that the seven candlesticks represent the seven churches. Candlesticks in themselves do not give light. They are holders of candles that do give light. The church of the Lord Jesus Christ does not have any light of its own. You and I are members of that church. We do not have any light. Jesus said, "I am the light of the world" (John 8:12). He also said, "As long as I am in the world, I am the light of the world" (John 9:5). Then He said to His followers, "Ye are the light of the world" (Matt. 5:14), suggesting that, after He left, His own light would shine through them out in a dark world.

LIGHT VERSUS LIGHT-BEARERS

The best illustration I can give is that of the sun and the moon. You look into the sky in the daytime and you see the sun; at nighttime, you see the moon, just like the sun—not as bright, but nevertheless giving off light, but not its own light. The moon has no light of its own as you well know. The only light the moon has, it gets from the sun. The moon is a mirror, a reflector. When the sun has descended below the horizon, and the moon is overhead, you don't see the sun, but you see the moon. The sun shines nevertheless against the moon. Out there in space (238,000 miles)—the moon is receiving the light from the sun and reflecting it to the earth. And we look, and we say, "What a beautiful moon!"

Likewise the Lord has gone out of sight, so to speak, since He has gone back to heaven, but His light shines through nonetheless. He is reflected to the world through us as the world looks at us. We, therefore, are the light of the world, but we don't have any light of our own. If we will remember that, it will help us to keep from being proud. Because we don't really have anything to boast about. We are dead in trespasses and sins. We have no righteousness of our own. Our righteousness is as filthy rags. Get rid of them, burn them—filthy! Yet that is all we have; it is all we are. But, in Christ . . . ah, that is different! In Him we have everything. In Him we live and move and have our being.

We must realize we have nothing, and we are nothing apart from Him. Our very breath is in His hands. Your heart is ticking away, and time is rapidly running out. One time, the Lord will say, "That's it!" He knows which will be our last heartbeat. And in that moment, there will be no appeal.

I am trying to say, we are absolutely, totally helpless, totally depraved, totally unlovely, totally unworthy, and totally without any ability or any worth in and of ourselves. Nevertheless, isn't it marvelous that He loved us enough to die for us, that He gave to us His own righteousness, and now He allows us to be in the world and shine forth, reflecting His light to others. That is why He told us we were the light of the world. That is amazing!

The Bible says: "Let your light so shine before men, that they may see your good works, and glorify your Father . . ." (Matt. 5:16). Not you, but your Father which is in heaven.

If there is anything that makes us sick, it is when preachers, evangelists and laymen, doing the work of the Lord, want to get all the credit for themselves. Well, Christ is in the middle of His church—all one church. He is the light. We are the light-bearers. It is our job to let His light shine through us. This requires the power of the Holy Spirit.

Now we come to

THE PORTRAIT OF CHRIST

I am sure that all of you have pictures of Christ in your homes. I wonder whether everybody realizes they are not from original snapshots. There were no Polaroid cameras in the days of Christ, and there are no artists, living or dead, who ever painted Christ after having seen Him. That is to say, all the pictures of Christ that are in existence today are merely the pure fiction of the mind—the result of the imagination of some individual as to what that individual thought Christ looked like.

I am not meaning to suggest that you go home and throw away all your pictures of Christ. I am suggesting that Christ today does not look anything like the pictures you have on your wall.

However, we are going to see His picture from the Word of God. John tells us what Christ really looks like. If any of you have artistic abilities, you might try painting an authentic portrait because it has never been done. Of course, before you get your expectations too high, I must warn you, it is impossible! That is why it has never been done. You shall see in a moment why this is true. Christ, today, in His glorified person in heaven above, seated at the Father's right hand, is so wonderful, so majestic, so glorious, so brilliant, that no earthly canvas or film could possibly capture His portrait. No earthly artist could possibly paint the picture of the heavenly Christ.

WHAT DID CHRIST LOOK LIKE?

It may be that the pictures you have are not too far from what Christ looked like when He was here—who can tell? We really do not know much about what He looked like when He was here on earth. We know a few things. We know that He wore a beard—because the Bible refers to the fact that they would pluck the hair from His beard. But that does not tell you very much. We can say Christ was not particularly attractive when He was here. He bore the burden of sin, so that His face was marred.

Isaiah 53:2 tells us, ". . . he hath no form nor comeliness; and when we shall see him, there is no beauty that we should desire him. . . ." Possibly because of the tremendous burden of sin that was upon Him, He did not appear attractive to men. But all of that is changed now as we shall see. Now He is "altogether lovely."

Personally, I think Jesus was a tall man. In the Garden Tomb in Jerusalem where I believe Jesus was actually laid, there is a place chiseled out of the rock which I think has a story to tell. There is a stone ledge at the one end where the head would have been and, of course, the feet would have been at the other end. Now, the area where the body is laid is just a little lower than the rest of the tomb. Imagine two levels in the tomb, the door being in the higher level. The Bible says John outran Peter and got to the tomb first. He looked in the door toward the place where the body had laid, but he did not notice the head clothes. He could not see them. The spot was below the ledge and out of sight. But when Peter came later on and dashed into the tomb, he came in and saw the head clothes. One must actually go inside the tomb to see the place where the head would have been.

But the interesting thing to me is that at the place where the feet would have been, you can notice that the rock was chiseled away in a rough manner, indicating that they were in a hurry to lengthen the space. Apparently, Joseph of Arimathea, whose tomb it was, was a short man, and the tomb was prepared for him. Suddenly, they used it for Christ, and it was not long enough. So quickly, in a rough, hurried manner, they chiseled away the rock. Now the fascinating thing is this. I am six feet, two inches, and I stretched out myself on my back, right on the spot where I think the body of Christ lay. As far as I could tell, for me, they would not have needed to chisel away any rock. So I'm assuming Jesus was a tall man.

Now please, don't ask for chapter and verse. There aren't any. I am speculating. It's interesting, but let's get away from speculation and let's get back to the Biblical account.

John says in verses 12 and 13:

> And I turned to see the voice that spake with me. And being turned, I saw seven golden candlesticks; And in the midst of the seven candlesticks one like unto the Son of man. . . .

Now here is the question—how is John going to describe the person of Christ? We are going to have the actual description of this magnificent person—wonderful beyond words. But we shall discover that words are totally inadequate.

LANGUAGE IS INADEQUATE

I told you that even though you might be a wonderful artist, you couldn't possibly paint the picture that is here presented. Now, I must say, no matter how good you are with words, you cannot do it with words either; that is, not adequately. John wasn't writing in English; he was writing in Greek. But neither the Greek nor the English is sufficient, and the Chinese language wouldn't be any better. There is no language on earth that is adequate and sufficient to describe the splendor and the glory and the magnificence of the person of Jesus Christ as He appears today if you could see Him in heaven.

But nevertheless words are the only means we have of communicating this account. So let's read what John says; then we will have to trust the Holy Spirit to use those words to get through to us and let us see the person of Christ. That's the best we can do. After all, the Bible says: "Eye hath not seen, nor ear heard, neither have entered into the heart of man, the things that God hath prepared for them that love him . . ." (I Cor. 2:9). And one of those things is just to look at the face of the Lord and adore Him. But we must never quote that verse without quoting the next one also: "But God hath revealed them unto us by his Spirit." We must take time to allow the Holy

Spirit to show us that which can be seen in no other way.

Now, there is something that is a pet peeve with me, and I don't know how to change it. From my own personal experience, I have found that it is not possible to sit down and read through ten verses and during that time have the Holy Spirit open up the whole vista of heaven. We are still too full of things of earth.

SPIRITUAL RESULTS REQUIRE TIME

For years, I wondered why it seemed so much easier to get a real demonstration of the presence and the power of the Holy Spirit in camp with the young people at the end of a week than it was to get the same kind of results in an hour or two in a church service. But I know the answer now. When those youngsters come to camp, they leave the things of the world at home—many of them, at least, if not all. The television set is left at home and so are a lot of other influences that hinder spiritual growth. The first thing that usually happens when they get up in the morning is prayer, followed by a Bible lesson. Then they go to classes, one after the other. They have recreation with Christian supervision in a Christian atmosphere. They don't hear any cursing and swearing and probably no nagging or fighting. The last thing at night before they go to bed is prayer. After a week of this the Lord can pour out His Spirit in marvelous power.

CAMP IDRAHAJE

I saw that happen in a manner that still thrills me when I think about it. High in the Rockies, there is a camp called "Idrahaje." Any of you familiar with that place? Well, the man who started that camp simply took the song "I'd Rather Have Jesus" and took the first syllable of each word, put them together and called it "Camp Idrahaje." I was invited there to give a Bible lesson each night to the young people.

It was kind of a rough camp. They had some Americans from New Mexico who were pretty tough. During the beginning of the week we had some problems. Some of those fellows swaggered in wearing their cowboy boots, determined they weren't going to do what they were told to do. They didn't want to participate in camp activities. So a couple of boys sat in their cabins and decided they were going to do only what *they* wanted to do. The director of the camp, who was a pastor and a good friend of mine, knew I had been a schoolteacher and a principal, so he handed some responsibility over to me and said, "How about going up and getting those boys out?" Well, I was a schoolteacher in the days when teachers could be teachers and pupils were pupils. I don't think I could teach today with pupils wanting to be boss. But anyway, I and one of the other pastors, a fellow schoolteacher, went up to the boys' bunkhouse.

I said: "Now you boys are not going to put up any argument, because we are going out there, and you are going to participate, and that is that." We took the boys bodily and marched them out to join the group. Well, they participated. That was the end of the initial rebellion.

FAITH TO STOP THE RAIN

And during that week there was a gradual mellowing. I would say about half of the campers that week were unsaved. Some of them, as I have indicated, thought they were pretty tough hombres—you know what I mean! The last night of the meeting came when we would ordinarily have had the campfire service— you are familiar with that, I'm sure. Well, that night it rained. The devil didn't want any service that night, I am sure, but the Lord got the victory. We retreated from the campfire to the largest building they had. It was covered with a tin roof. It rained so hard, the rain on the roof made it difficult to be heard. But I gave the message, and as I finished, it really started to pour. I didn't have the faith to pray and ask the Lord to stop the rain but the director of the camp did. He got up and started praying that the Lord would stop the rain. And the rain stopped. It did, indeed!

Then I proceeded to give the invitation. First, there was one, then another came forward. Then another one! As we continued the invitation, slowly but surely boys and girls were coming to the front to acknowledge Christ as Saviour and Lord of their lives. And they kept coming. After a while, the presence of the Holy Spirit was so great, some of the youngsters who had been praying for their unsaved friends began to cry when they saw that their prayers were being answered. They wept for joy. After a while, practically everybody was shedding tears.

There were still about a half dozen of the toughest ones, boys and girls, who had not come. But now there was a lot of praying and there was a big group down front. We kept giving the invitation—no pressure—just inviting. Before the service was over every unsaved boy and girl that we knew about came walking down the aisle, including the boy that was the toughest of them all—he was sobbing like a child. That must have been the most embarrassing moment of his life. In the presence of all these young people before whom he paraded as such a tough fellow, he was sobbing in uncontrolled weeping as he came down the aisle to publicly receive Christ into his heart.

All this happened some years ago. But recently I was out there in New Mexico preaching, and this boy came to the meetings. He was now a tall, handsome young man. He had come home from the university where he was studying. I asked him: "Do you still love the Lord; are you saved?"

He said, "Yes, I am." And he insisted that since it wasn't possible for him to take me to his home, he would take me to a restaurant. He wanted to buy me a meal. What a pleasant experience that was!

I am trying to tell you that if you would have the Holy Spirit show you the deep things of God, an extended period of time is necessary. You have got to get alone with the Lord, shut out things of the world, and let the Holy Spirit minister to you as you meditate. And then there will come a point if you saturate yourself enough with the Word, and with the Lord, and yield yourself particularly to the Holy Spirit, that He will indeed allow you to catch a glimpse of the glory world.

THE SON OF MAN

John says, "And in the midst of the seven candlesticks, one like unto the Son of man . . ."—that's interesting! Why didn't he say the Son of God. Here on earth, John was Jesus' closest earthly friend, the one who lay on Jesus' bosom the last night Jesus was alive before He went to the cross, the one to whom Jesus committed the care of His mother. John, when he wrote his Gospel, delighted to call Jesus the Son of God. Jesus was God! He made the whole universe, He was the Eternal Creator. "All things were made by him, and without him was not any thing made that was made" (John 1:3); yet He took special delight in associating Himself with the creatures that He had made, calling Himself the Son of man.

Roosevelt, when he was president, delighted to call himself a farmer though he was a wealthy millionaire and president of the greatest country in the world. Whenever he registered to vote, they asked him his occupation. He was President of the United States, but he registered as a farmer. It's a crude illustration. But Jesus, the very God of heaven, delighted to identify Himself with the human race. This was true because He loved us. He loved us far beyond anything we can ever imagine. He loved us with an everlasting love. It was that great love that sent Him to the cross in the body of a man so that we might have eternal life. And I believe that His reference to the Son of man is a reminder that He is our Saviour. So He delights to call Himself the Son of man, and here He directs John to write it thus. John saw "one like unto the Son of man, clothed with a garment down to the foot."

HIS GARMENTS

We shall talk about the garments we will wear in heaven when we get to chapter 19. The tendency in our present culture is toward fewer and fewer, and lesser and lesser, and skimpier and skimpier garments. But in heaven we will not be naked. In heaven we will be fully clothed. The Lord here is wearing garments down to the foot and girded about the paps with a golden girdle. We really don't know too much about the garments the Lord will wear. We shall see when He goes on His honeymoon in chapter 19, He will be dressed in red. You can be sure His garments will be far more attractive than any suits, dresses, gowns or uniforms ever made on earth.

HIS HAIR

But now notice, it says: "His head and his hairs were white like wool," but that isn't sufficient lest you picture the fleece of a sheep. So He added, "as white as snow." That brings up an interesting subject. When we get to heaven, will we have the same color of hair we have now? The answer is: I don't know. I am sorry to disappoint you. There are a lot of places where it is best to say, "I don't know," and I don't know why we should be ashamed to admit we don't know. After all, there isn't anybody here who is God. Only God knows all the answers, and the Bible really doesn't tell us everything. Someone described Christ as having black hair. Here, it says His hair is white. Could it be that we can change it at will, without even dyeing it? I don't know. I am sure of one thing—heaven will be a beautiful place filled with beautiful things. If you have seen a lovely head of hair here, you haven't seen anything compared to what you are going to see when you get to heaven.

I'm sure we'll have a full head of hair, too. There will be no bald heads in heaven. I know that because the Bible says, in effect, "Don't worry about what happens to you, even if you are put to death; in due time, when the books are settled, not a hair on your head will be missing." That used to seem like a paradox to me, but Jesus was simply saying that even if you lose your scalp, you will not be missing one hair when you get to heaven and the accounts are settled. And of course that is good news to me. They tell me I had about a hundred thousand to start. I haven't counted them lately, but there are a few missing as you can see. When we get to heaven, we'll all have a full head of hair again.

John looks at Christ and starts by describing His hair. He says "white like wool," but realizing that is inadequate, he adds another phrase, "as white as snow." I am sure he realizes that it is still inadequate, but what more can he say?

And, of course, white suggests purity. But I am not going to spend much time "figurizing," spiritualizing or symbolizing because we don't have any instructions telling us how to do it. Some people are good at that; I am not. I like to read the Bible and say, "That's what it says." Certainly Christ is the essence of purity. He is the Holy One. He is the one who is altogether perfect. He never committed any sin. Perhaps this fact is portrayed by the appearance of His hair. I'm sure of one thing: We'll know and understand some of these things much better when we get to heaven.

Now the last part of verse 14: "And His eyes were as a flame of fire."

HIS EYES

Perhaps some of you are still hoping that you might use your artistic ability to paint a picture of Christ and turn out a masterpiece. But now you will be forced to give up. How are you going to paint the eyes of Christ when John says they are like flames of fire. If you tried to paint that you would have a monstrosity. But John saw no monstrosity; he was looking at the One who is altogether lovely.

Think what the Bible has to say about the eyes of Christ. It says that His eyes run to and fro upon the earth in search of a man whose heart is right toward Him. When we look out into distant space, we must use telescopes; we can't see very far with the natural eye. But the eyes of the Lord can see all the way from heaven to earth. According to the Bible, Christ ascended above all powers and principalities which, to me, means He went beyond the very last star. That must, of necessity, mean more than ten billion light-years away. Yet the Bible says He can look down to earth and, of course, He doesn't use a telescope to look through all that space. He looks right into the heart of every man! "Man looketh on the outward appearance, but the Lord looketh on the heart" (I Sam. 16:7). Imagine the power of the eyes of the Lord. He can see our faults. He can see our thoughts and our motives. He can see everything we are. In the day or in the dark, there is nothing hid from Him. Everything we are, everything we feel, everything we think, every motive, every desire . . . He can see it all. And He is searching for a man whose heart is right toward Him.

He found some men like that in past history. I wonder how many He finds today. Daniel was one of those men. The Lord loved him very much. In heaven he had the reputation of being the man on earth that was greatly loved in heaven. David was one of those men, in spite of his sins. He was a man after God's own heart.

Well, there it is, totally inadequate—but that is what John says. That is the best he can do: "His eyes were as a flame of fire."

HIS FEET

Now take a look at verse 15, "And his feet like unto fine brass." Try to picture that! If you think of the feet of some brass image, you are all wrong. That is totally too earthly. So John adds ". . . as if they burned in a furnace . . ." and I don't know if that helps much . . . feet like fine brass as if they burned in a furnace!

I realize the Bible speaks of brass symbolically in connection with judgment. It says in chapter 19 that when the Lord comes, He shall tread the winepress of the wrath and fierceness of Almighty God. So He does come in judgment, but I don't think John is thinking of judgment here. John sees Christ in person and he is just trying to tell us what he saw. And so he says that His eyes were like a flame of fire, and His feet were like polished, beautiful brass. That isn't quite sufficient, so he adds, as if they were burning in a furnace. That is only part of the picture. The Holy Spirit will have to let you see the rest. This is the magnificent person of the glorified Christ. John saw Him and one day soon we shall see Him, too, in person.

HIS VOICE

Verse 15 gives us the description of His voice. What do you think the voice of God would be like? How could you describe it? Those of you who never met me before I came to this service . . . you heard my name and you saw my picture on the card, you wondered what Nathan Meyer sounded like, now didn't you?

I have had the experience myself of hearing about a preacher and wondering what his voice would sound like if I could hear him speak. I missed hearing many of the great Bible preachers of the first half of the twentieth century because I got into evangelical circles too late. I read their books and I feel like I know them and have known them for a long time, but I never really met them and so I never heard them. I am talking about men like Dr. C. I. Scofield, Dr. William Pettingill, Dr. Harry Ironside, and others.

Harry Ironside was to me one of the greatest and dearest saints of God of this century. I read the story of his life "Ordained of the Lord" about the time he died, and I read his articles in the *Sunday School Times*. So I felt like I knew him very well. When I heard of his death, I regretted the fact that I had never had the privilege of hearing him. I wondered what his voice sounded like.

Late one night I was driving down the Oklahoma Turnpike heading toward my next speaking engagement. I was listening to a religious broadcast coming out of Texas. I was getting a little drowsy, but all of a sudden I woke up fast. I heard the announcer say: "Now we are going to listen to a message by the late Dr. Ironside." I was wide awake as I listened. And I was delighted. He had a beautiful voice. It was deep, rich and resonant and I was pleased. Praise God for tape recorders.

Now think, what would the voice of the Lord Jesus sound like if you could hear what John heard? After all, He is God. It was His voice that spoke and the very stars took their places in the universe. Some day His voice will speak and His enemies will die. "Out of his mouth goeth a sharp sword, that with it he should smite the nations" (Rev. 19:15). The sword is His word. He will simply speak; that is all it will take, and they will die. Such a powerful voice! What will it sound like?

John says at the end of verse 15, "And his voice as the sound of many waters." I have pondered long as to what that might mean. Many waters! Great rushing torrents of water! Listen to the powerful, penetrating roar, the rumble and the roll of the mighty Niagara! Tons and tons of water crashing over the cliff, striking the rocky gorge far below, sending out the sound of the falls for miles around! And nobody can stop it. Nobody can turn it off!

So it is when God speaks. John heard the voice of God and he said that it was like the sound of many waters. Meditate on that! The Holy Spirit will do the rest.

One day when our son, Paul, was just a little fellow, possibly three or four, we had a severe thunderstorm. We were living in Winona Lake, Indiana. It thundered and the whole house rattled. He was afraid. So I said: "Now, Paul, don't be afraid. That is God speaking." That was intriguing to his little boyish mind, and as boys will do, he asked a question: "What is God saying?"

I had to think fast. Then I said, "Well, He is saying, 'All you little people down there on earth, listen to Me, this is God. I am speaking! You can't turn Me off. You can't forget about Me— can't deny that I am here. I am God. You must listen.' " After that, Paul seemed fascinated by the thunder. God was speaking!

The Bible tells us He thunders with His voice; He speaks in the thunder. This is expressed several times in the Bible. One day God is going to speak so the thunder will roll around the globe, and nobody will be able to turn it off. His voice is powerful like the sound of many waters. What a voice! Of course, He speaks in the still, small voice, too. And with great love He invites sinners to Himself.

We are ready now for verse 16.

And he had in his right hand seven stars: and out of his mouth went a sharp twoedged sword: and his countenance was as the sun shineth in his strength.

PROPER INTERPRETATION OF SCRIPTURE

Before we can understand a verse like this, we must decide whether to interpret it literally or figuratively. I believe in taking the Bible literally unless there is some Biblical reason, mixed with a little common sense, indicating otherwise. I have found that formula to be the only one that works.

HIS SWORD

Now there is a Biblical reason, and common sense will confirm it, for not putting a blade of steel between the teeth of the Lord Jesus. The Bible says that His word is the sword and it is sharper than any blade of steel, because it can separate, not only the head from the shoulders like a blade of steel, but it can separate the body and the spirit and the soul. No earthly sword can do that! His sword is His word. The Bible is the written Word. When Jesus speaks it is the spoken Word. But He in person is the living Word. Here we are speaking of the word that comes out of His mouth: "Out of His mouth went a sharp twoedged sword. . . ."

HIS FACE

"And his countenance was as the sun shineth in his strength." How is John going to describe the face of His Majesty, THE KING OF KINGS, THE LORD OF LORDS, THE ALMIGHTY CREATOR, Himself? The one who made the whole universe! He made every sunset and every rose, everything that is beautiful, everything! He made it! How beautiful He Himself must be! The Bible says He is altogether lovely, and John is now going to tell us about His face. We shall discover in chapter 22 that when we get to heaven, we shall see His face! And we will bow down before Him. We will adore Him; we will worship Him!

ADORATION AND WORSHIP

He will be so lovely, so beautiful, so attractive, we will constantly sit and stare at Him, but it will not be staring as we do here below. It will be adoration and He will not be embarrassed. He will desire and deserve our adoration. For He is worthy. So we shall look on His face, and John here is trying to describe that face. It seems to me that this passage reaches a climax at this point. Earthly words in an earthly language are not sufficient to describe the wonder, the glory, and the beauty of the person of Christ. John tells us His face is radiant like the noonday sun . . . that's all he can say, so John lets it go at that.

The Bible says that when we get to heaven, there will be no need of the sun, because the Lord is the light thereof. This is mysterious. The sun is so brilliant that we cannot look at it with our natural eyes for more than just a few seconds even though it is 93 million miles away, and yet the Lord Jesus is going to be more brilliant than the sun. And we are going to stand right in front of Him and look at His face. From His person will emanate the light that will light the whole of God's heaven. And we are going to be awe-struck with His beauty. We will lovingly gaze upon His face as we worship and adore Him forever! John says His countenance, that is His face, was as the sun shining in all its strength.

And now we are not surprised that John says in verse 17: "And when I saw him, I fell at his feet as dead." John prostrates himself before the living Christ in worship and adoration. Remember, John was Jesus' closest earthly friend. He hadn't seen Him since the ascension nearly 70 years ago. Now he sees Him again.

If men had described this, they would have had a reunion of two long lost buddies. But it is not so. God is God, John is a mere mortal. John falls down on his face before God, but Jesus in love and compassion, laid His right hand upon John saying, "Fear not." John had heard His voice in the flesh long ago say: "Be of good cheer; it is I, be not afraid" (Matt. 14:27). The waves had been roaring on the sea of Galilee. The wind was rocking the water and the boat was tossing. The disciples were afraid the ship would sink and they would all be drowned. But everything changed when Jesus said: "It is I, be not afraid."

Jesus calmed the rolling sea and it became smooth as glass and the disciples marveled. Isn't it thrilling? It speaks of the fact that all of creation obeys Him precisely, except fallen angels and sinful men. The wind and the waves obey His voice, but man rebels.

Well, John hears these pleasant words. "Fear not." Jesus is saying, "Don't be afraid, John. I am the first and the last. I am He that liveth." (He was dead, but now He is alive.) So He says, "I am he that liveth, and was dead; and, behold, I am alive for evermore. Amen!" Which means: So be it, Lord. Then Jesus continues, ". . . and have the keys of hell [hades] and of death." Hades is a place of conscious torment where all the lost of all ages go at death to await the last judgment. Death is the gateway that ushers them into that place.

By the same token, death to the saints is precious in the Lord's sight, because it is the gateway to heaven and the Lord has the keys to both places. I trust that every person here has put his faith and trust in Christ. If so, you haven't got a thing to worry about. Christ is the mighty God, and someday soon we shall see Him as John saw Him—in person. Then we shall prostrate ourselves before Him and we shall look upon His face and we shall exclaim, "Thou art worthy, O Lord, to receive glory and honour and power . . . for thou wast slain, and hast redeemed us to God by thy blood out of every kindred, and tongue, and people, and nations" (Rev. 4:11; 5:9).

May the Holy Spirit Himself enable us to catch a glimpse of this glorious person even now. And as that happens we shall bow before Him in loving adoration and praise as we worship Him in spirit and in truth.

LET US PRAY

Our Heavenly Father, we thank Thee for this wonderful Book. We praise Thee for the way in which Thou dost provide for our information so that we should not be left ignorant concerning the future and the things of heaven. We know that by divine inspiration holy men of old wrote as they were guided and guarded by the Holy Spirit Himself. And we thank Thee that it is so. We thank Thee that we have the Bible freely available. We thank Thee for the privilege of studying it. We thank Thee for the Holy Spirit who delights to make these things plain to our hearts. We thank Thee for the joy we experience when we meditate upon the wonders of our God.

We pray that each of us may get homesick for heaven, homesick for Christ as we study the Word and contemplate the glory that shall be ours when we shall pass through those portals of pearl and walk down those streets of gold and look upon the face of Him who is altogether lovely, even Jesus Christ our Saviour, our Lord and our Coming King. In His blessed name, we pray. Amen!

Part Two

The Things
Which Are (Now)

II

The Church
on Earth

REVELATION 2 and 3

Our message tonight deals with the story of the Church Age here on earth. It is really the history of the whole Church Age from Pentecost to the second coming of Christ written in advance. That's prophecy. So we sometimes call it the church in prophecy and history.

We are dealing now with Part II of Jesus' outline given in chapter 1, verse 19—"the things which are [now]."

In our next message we will begin with chapter 4 dealing with things which shall be hereafter. But right now we want to study "things which are" now—this present age—as revealed in chapters 2 and 3.

HISTORY AND PROPHECY

We have here seven letters written to seven historical churches but it is important to remember that we also have a book of prophecy. In the first verse of chapter 1 we were told that the purpose of this book was to show his servants *things which must shortly come to pass.* That's prophecy.

Since it is a book of prophecy, we are going to look for a prophetic message. Living in the twentieth century, we have an advantage over Christians of all previous centuries because we can check up on John and see just how it turned out. As John wrote this prophecy near the end of the first century he was looking ahead. We are living nearly twenty centuries later and we are looking back. We can put the history of the last two thousand years along side of John's prophecy to see how they compare. This is very important because if John's prophecy was actually fulfilled up to this point, we have a right to expect that the rest will follow likewise just as John wrote it.

So let me begin with chapter 2 now and show you the letters here written to seven historic churches in John's day. After that we'll deal with the prophetic element.

SEVEN CHURCHES AND SEVEN LETTERS

The first one is to Ephesus. Notice verse 1, "unto the angel of the church of *Ephesus.*" See verse 8, "unto the angel of the church of *Smyrna*"—that is the second church. In verse 12 "to the angel of the church in *Pergamos*." In verse 18 "unto the angel of the church in *Thyatira*." Now look in chapter 3, verse 1, "unto the angel of the church in *Sardis*." In verse 7 "unto the angel of the church in *Philadelphia*," and finally the seventh one in the fourteenth verse "unto the angel of the church of the *Laodiceans*."

So there you have seven letters dictated by the Lord Himself to John to be delivered to the seven churches which he had selected. Seven is the number indicating totality. Seven days make the total week. So God is here using seven churches to picture the whole period of Christendom. We will see seven periods of church history constituting the whole church age. Each church has a particular problem, each has a peculiar relationship to the Lord and each church is carefully described. Each one is both historic and prophetic.

These seven are given in a specific order so that while these letters were originally written to seven historic churches and delivered to those churches, God was really prophetically picturing seven periods of church history. I shall try briefly to show you how it works out. I wish we had about four or five hours, but we don't. So you listen fast, I will talk fast, and we'll get through in due time. I won't deal with all of them in detail but enough to give you the overall picture.

I want to begin by showing you that in each of these seven letters, the Lord presents seven things. He loves to use the number seven. In the Book of Revelation it is used more than 50 times. So it is appropriate that in each letter we should have seven things.

1. THE NAME OF THE CHURCH

First of all you will find the *name* of the church. There is a letter being addressed and so it is appropriate it should be addressed to the person or group receiving the letter. In this case it is the Church of Ephesus.

2. THE IDENTIFICATION OF THE AUTHOR

In the second case, you have the author identified: "These things saith he that holdeth the seven stars in his right hand, who walketh in the midst of the seven golden candlesticks." To know who that is, you have to look in chapter 1, verse 20: "... the seven candlesticks which thou sawest are the seven churches." The one who is speaking there is the Lord. He is the One who is standing in the midst of His church. This is a reference to the Lord Himself. In every case, the description of the author is different, but in each case, the author is the same. It is Christ every time. But the description of Christ is always significant in view of the condition of the church.

3. JESUS KNOWS

Verse 2 gives us the third thing that we find in every letter, and it is unique. It is simply the words "I know." He didn't have to tell them He knows. He could have proceeded to tell them what He knows as He will do next, but He didn't. He started by saying, I want you to know that *I know* your condition.

Let me run through them quickly and point them out. In verse 2 to Ephesus, "I know"; in verse 9 to Smyrna, "I know"; in verse 13 to Pergamos, "I know"; in verse 19 to Thyatira, "I know"; in chapter 3, verse 1, to Sardis, "I know"; to Philadelphia in verse 8, "I know"; and finally to Laodicea in verse 15, "I know." Seven times, once in each letter, to each church, He says, "I know." I think this is significant. The Lord wants us never to forget that He knows all about us. This works two ways. It covers the negative and the positive.

A. The Positive Side

First of all, let's say you are trying your best to yield yourself to the Holy Spirit and to do the Lord's will. Perhaps you are not succeeding entirely, but you are trying very hard to please the Lord in whatever place He has put you with whatever talent He has given you—you are trying to please the Lord. But some of the folks around you don't appreciate your efforts. Maybe even the pastor doesn't appreciate you. Maybe some of the church officers don't appreciate you. Somebody along the way, perhaps, says something untrue and very unkind. It may be something very nasty and mean. Suddenly you are very discouraged and you are prone to say: "Well, if that's the way they feel, I'll quit." Now you ought not to do that, you ought to remember *the Lord knows*.

My father was elected to the free ministry by his congregation when he was just a young man (the same way in which I got into the ministry). He had a farm; he taught school; he worked in a bank; and thus he earned a living. But all his life he served as a leader of the church. They didn't call him pastor, but he was the elder-in-charge and he preached regularly and was responsible for conducting the affairs of the church, and so forth.

Now some of the people in the church, from time to time, were very unkind in some of the things they said. I remember when some disgruntled church members came to our house and in language that was very un-Christlike and very unkind, criticized my father for something he had done or had not done, as the case may be. It was something with which they disagreed, of course. I remember on more than one occasion like that when my father was feeling very discouraged, my mother would say, "Well, I'm glad the Lord knows. I'm glad the Lord knows."

I have never forgotten that. It has been valuable to me many times. Somebody may have said something about us that is entirely untrue. They misjudged our motives. They may have been sincere in doing so but nevertheless it was quite cutting and very unkind and very untrue. The best thing we can say at a time like that is, "Well, I'm glad the Lord knows." And the Lord wants us to know that He knows; so He reminds us seven times that He knows.

B. The Negative Side

Now, by the same token, if there is sin in our lives and we are trying to hide it from those around us, it is good to remember the Lord says, "I know."

Some of these churches were in the one category; some were in the other; the Lord knows both sides. So if you become discouraged while you are trying to do the best you can, because somebody doesn't appreciate your efforts, then just remember the Lord knows and He will take care of it. If on the other hand you are hiding your sins, then you must remember, the Lord knows and He wants you to know that He knows.

4. THE CONDITION OF THE CHURCH

The fourth thing you will find is the actual thing that He knows: the condition of the church. Follow in your Bible as I read, beginning with verse 2. "I know thy works, and thy labour, and thy patience, and how thou canst not bear them which are evil: and thou hast tried them which say they are apostles, and are not, and hast found them liars: And hast borne, and hast patience, and for my name's sake hast laboured, and hast not fainted." That is the good side that He knows. Now the other side: "Nevertheless I have somewhat against thee, because thou hast left thy first love." This church here is something less than 70 years old and it has already started to grow cold. I know some churches that are a lot less than 70 years old and have grown cold, too. They still have a lot of good points but they don't put the Lord first as they should because they aren't quite as much in love with Him anymore as when they were first saved.

This is a problem for each of us, individually; we must constantly struggle against it. We must draw close to the Lord, feed upon His Word and exercise in the things of the Spirit. If we do this, we will learn to love Him more and more. Our love for Him will grow greater and stronger with every passing day. But if we neglect our spiritual feasting, our spiritual exercising, our close walk with the Lord and our fellowship with Him, we will eventually discover we will have left that first love. This is the biggest problem we Christians face, and it is the big problem every church faces.

5. THE REFERENCE TO HIS COMING

The fifth thing that we find in this letter is a reference to the Second Coming. Verse 5 says: "Remember therefore from whence thou art fallen, and repent, and do the first works; or else *I will come.*" However, there is one church in whose letter the Lord did not refer to His coming, but He referred to their coming to Him—that is the church of the martyrs, the church of Smyrna. They were going to die and come to Him. But in every other letter you will find the fifth thing is a reference to His coming: "I will come."

6. AN INVITATION TO HEAR

The sixth thing to which I call your attention is in verse 7: "He that hath an ear, let him hear." Now that sounds strange. Maybe some of you had to rush to church tonight. You got home from work and you were in a hurry. You ate supper, piled the dishes in the sink and hurried to get here in time for the service. In the rush perhaps you forgot your glasses or maybe you forgot your purse. Maybe you even forgot your teeth. But nobody forgot his ears. I see everybody is wearing his, so why did the Lord say what He did? It almost sounds foolish until you read the rest of the verse. "He that hath an ear, let him hear what the Spirit saith unto the churches."

Ah, that is different. This is not the ear with which you hear the voice of the Spirit. The voice of God doesn't necessarily come to you through the audible ear. The Lord may use an audible voice to reach the ear of the heart, but not necessarily so. At any rate, when the Spirit speaks to you, He gets down inside where He can speak to the heart. What Jesus is saying is this: Those who have the Holy Spirit within and are listening to Him speak, let them hear what the Spirit is saying. That is the essence.

A LOVE LETTER

This book was not written to unsaved individuals. Remember in chapter 1, verse 1, it was written to show His servants things which must shortly happen. This is a love letter from the Lord to you. He wants you to have a special message and He wrote much of it in code. Well, then, you say, "I can't understand it." Oh, not so fast! If you really love the Lord, you will be studying the Bible from cover to cover and you will discover the Lord has hung keys here and there which you will find as you read. Those keys will unlock other doors that seem, at first, to be difficult. This book was written for God's children who love Him enough to really study it. In so doing, they will find the Holy Spirit delights to be their teacher. These things are spiritually discerned. Carnal man cannot simply breeze through the Bible expecting to satisfy his own intellectual curiosity concerning the future history of this world without any desire to learn any spiritual truth. God does not cast His pearls before swine.

A few of you are just young enough to remember the day when you received a letter, the very handwriting of which made your heart begin to beat a little faster. You know what I am talking about. Oh, they don't write love letters anymore? Well, some of you got them in your day, and you know what I mean. Now, when you received those letters, they were just for you; they were not for the public. You didn't dash down to the post office and tack them up on the bulletin board. Of course not! Why didn't you? You would have been proud, perhaps, to do so, but you know that everybody who would have come in would have read that letter and laughed. If God had written in plain language what He wanted to tell His children, many of the people of the world would laugh.

SPIRITUAL DISCERNMENT

I think God wrote Revelation to be largely closed to carnal man, but it is wide open to those who love the Lord. He that has a spiritual ear, let him hear what the Spirit is saying to the churches. I have never yet found a person who was sincerely looking for the truth and who was willing to listen to the exposition of this book who then said, "I can't understand it." I have never yet met such a person and I have preached through this book more than a hundred times. God guarantees a special blessing to those who will study it, and He says: He that hath a spiritual ear, let him hear. And the Spirit is saying: These things are spiritually discerned.

You may have all the degrees that all the universities in the whole wide world could offer but if you do not have the Holy Spirit to present to you the truth which is Christ, you can read through this book and learn almost nothing except one thing: judgment is facing you sometime in the future. That is about all the carnal man can learn. Judgment is plain enough but many of the other things he will skip because he won't know what it is all about.

But the individual who loves the Lord and studies the book from cover to cover will find the more he studies, the deeper it gets and the more it unfolds and the more wonderful it becomes. I get more thrilled every time I go through it. I would like to have a year with nothing to do but to go out somewhere on a lonely island like the remote shores of Hawaii and just study the Book of Revelation. There are so many things that have a relationship to the rest of the Bible and you don't learn these things by sitting down and reading ten verses at a time. You have to spend hours, shutting out the things of the world and making yourself available to the Holy Spirit; then He begins to let you see these things. After while you will hear the music of heaven; you will catch a glimpse of that glory-land and you will burst into tears. It is so wonderful!

I am trying to tell you that here we are expounding a precious love letter that God wants all His children to understand. The Holy Spirit will make it plain. "He that hath an ear, let him hear what the Spirit saith unto the churches."

7. THE REWARD

There is one more thing that we find in each of these letters. Number seven is the mention of the reward: "To him that overcometh will I give to eat of the tree of life, which is in the midst of the paradise of God." In every letter the reward is different but the reward is significant in view of the experience of the particular church.

Now you have a basis for study. You can take each of these letters and find the seven things we mentioned above with, of course, the single exception noted.

THE PROPHETIC MEANING –
SEVEN PERIODS OF CHURCH HISTORY

1. THE EPHESUS PERIOD – FIRST CENTURY

We discover that the description of the church of Ephesus pretty well describes Christendom as a whole during the first century.

2. THE SMYRNA PERIOD – A.D. 100 - 300

Let us move on now to Smyrna in verse 8. I want to show you that prophetically the description of Smyrna beautifully describes Christendom as a whole for two hundred years—from A.D. 100-300, so this was all future to John. To us, it is now history. It is a tremendous story.

Look at verse 8: "Unto the angel of the church in Smyrna . . . ." Smyrna was called the most beautiful city in Asia, and today it is the largest of all the seven cities, the only one with an airport. It is located in Turkey today and they call it Izmir.

As one approaches the city at night, coming down from the north, along the Turkish coast, one can see the lights of the city across the bay and it is a beautiful sight. The city is located on the slope of a high hill and the lights from the waterfront up to the citadel are a picture to behold. In the first century it was known as the most beautiful city of Asia.

Smyrna was also the name of a herb that gave off a fragrant aroma, but only when it was crushed. So it is appropriate that this church, located in a flourishing commercial city in the first century, should bear this name. For this was the church that was crushed, and in being crushed, it gave off a lovely fragrance to the nostrils of our God. Prophetically, this was the church of the martyrs for approximately 200 years. Let us read further:

"These things saith the first and the last." Do you see the significance of the description of Christ in view of the situation in which the church finds itself? This is the church of the martyrs when the Christians died by the thousands—many, many Christians giving their lives for their faith in Christ. Christ in speaking to them says: "These things saith the first and the last, which was dead and is alive; I know thy works, and tribulation, and poverty, (but thou art rich) . . . ."

Now that seems like a paradox, and we find such from time to time in this book. In one breath Jesus is saying to this church that He knows all about their troubles and trials and tribulations and poverty, but He says, "Don't worry, you are really very rich."

How can we explain that? I think I can give you an illustration that will help you to understand. Let's say that I am a very poor person. I own nothing. I don't even know where the next meal is coming from. I am absolutely penniless and destitute. Let's say that you are a Philadelphia lawyer settling the estate of a rich uncle of mine who has just left me a million dollars. You have been hunting me a long time and now at last you found me. Am I rich or poor? Look at my rags and empty pockets and I am poor. But look at the check in your hand with my name on it made out for a million dollars and I am rich. For the moment I am poor but as soon as I can get my hands on that check and get to a bank, I'll be rich.

Those who love the Lord here on this side of glory, no matter how poor they may be in this world, will be very, very wealthy when they get over there. So it was in the Smyrna period. They were willing to lay everything they had on the altar of sacrifice for the Lord, and Jesus assured them something like this: "I know your suffering. I know your tribulation, I know your poverty. But don't worry about it. When you get to heaven you will be fabulously wealthy." You see, God doesn't settle the books on this side of heaven.

Now the rest of the line says: "I know the blasphemy of them which say they are Jews, and are not, but are of the synagogue of Satan." They belong to the church of the devil. In my opinion, this has to do with some individuals who operated a fifth column, so to speak, trying to learn the secrets of the catacombs. Under the city of Rome, and around the city, there are more than a thousand miles of underground tunnels called catacombs. They were dug chiefly by the early Christians. They were tunneled out in the form of a maze. You know what a maze is? The tunnels criss-cross going in every direction and one doesn't know whether he is going to come to a dead-end or whether the passageway will continue on through. They are deep in the earth, maybe 35 feet under the surface. The tunnels were cut out of soft stone forming hallways about three or four feet wide with the ceiling as high as one's head or it may be much higher in some places. One can walk along just so far and then he comes to a "cross road." It is totally dark down there without the lights, of course. If one didn't have a guide, he wouldn't know which way to go. And no matter which way he went, he would come to another cross-tunnel. Very quickly he would be lost. The catacombs were purposely dug that way.

The Christians knew the "combination" for going in and moving through these passageways deep into the catacombs. There they could bury their dead without fear of the Roman soldiers coming in to molest them. There they could hold their services including "love feasts." We conducted a service in one of those rooms on one occasion deep in the catacombs. There was no pulpit; there was no furniture, no organ, no pews. Lights, yes, but nothing more! No glass windows, just the hard, stone walls of the underground chapel and in the walls was the grim reminder that there were those who long ago gave their lives for their faith in Jesus Christ. We could see the niches in the wall where the Christians had been buried. In some cases the stone slab, used to close the grave, had fallen away and you could see some of the bones of those individuals resting there. That was quite an atmosphere for a service, believe me, but we had a wonderful time. The Lord was there in power and blessed.

Well, I was saying these Christians would go underground to

conduct their services, and to bury their dead so that the Roman soldiers couldn't find them. I think this is in reference to some who infiltrated the group trying to learn the combination to find out where they were and to ferret them out.

Now notice verse 10: "Fear none of those things which thou shalt suffer"—it was a suffering church—"behold, the devil shall cast some of you into prison, that ye shall be tried; and ye shall have tribulation ten days; be thou faithful unto death, and I will give thee a crown of life."

Let me tell you what happened. During the 200 years from about A.D. 100 to 300, which this letter prophetically describes, we have a period of ten waves of awful persecution— that could be translated ten periods—and that is exactly what happened.

From the throne of the Caesars, the Emperors of Rome (world dictators, if you please) went forth the decree ten different times to destroy the sect of the lowly Nazarene. No method was too cruel to be used against the defenseless Christians.

THE RACK

These were some of the methods that were used. The rack is a wheel about two feet wide and higher than my head. Imagine there is one standing here mounted on an axle. I am a second-century Christian with my ankles chained to the floor and my wrists chained to the wheel—the rack. A soldier is standing at the crank turning the wheel, one ratchet at a time, stretching my body farther and farther. If I recant and say I will give up Christianity and renounce Christ, I can go free. But if I refuse to do that, the wheel will be turned until my limbs are torn from their sockets. Thus, I would die with excruciating pain. Thousands of Christians died on the rack during the Smyrna period. Sometimes the rack was in the form of a bed but the result was the same.

THE STAKE

Another method that was used was to tie Christians to a post, pile wooden fagots around them and then fire the wood making burning torches out of them. Thousands of Christians were burned at the stake for their faith in Jesus Christ.

THE CAGE

Still another method that was used was to put them in an iron cage. The cage was just as wide as a man's shoulders and about three feet high. The Christian was doubled up with his knees against his chin and in that cramped position the body was jammed in and the door was closed. Then the cage was suspended over a street in Rome and the passing crowds jeered as they went by. The cage was allowed to remain there until the Christian recanted or until from starvation or exposure to the elements, he died. And many Christians died that torturous death.

BOILING OIL

Others were dipped in boiling oil. What a horrible way to die!

CRUCIFIXION

Many Christians were nailed to wooden crosses, crucified like Christ.

THE LIONS

Some were taken to the arena of the Circus Maximus or the Colosseum. The Colosseum held fifty thousand people. Every afternoon the Romans would gather there for pleasure and excitement—kicks we call it now. The gladiators would fight but when they didn't get rough enough and the people wanted more excitement, more violence—the Christians would be turned into the arena. The hungry lions that had not been fed for days were loosed into the arena while the crowds cheered. The lions tore the Christians, clawed and chewed them. Many Christians died in the jaws of the lions.

The devil used all the methods that he could concoct to try to stamp out the religion of Jesus Christ. For over 200 years in ten awful waves of persecution, Christians were martyred for their faith in Jesus Christ. The words of Jesus brought encouragement: "I know your poverty, I know your tribulation, I know your suffering, but don't worry; when you get to heaven, I will set it all straight. You will be fabulously wealthy and I will give you the crown of life."

Did this persecution stamp out Christianity? No, it did not. It did produce a pure church, and a pure church is a powerful church.

You see, whenever Christians were martyred, pagans watched and wondered. They couldn't understand the strange, mysterious behavior of Christians facing death. When pagans came to the place of execution they came cringing, begging, pleading, crying. But when the Christians came face to face with death, they came singing. They came with a smile. They came as a conqueror, not as the conquered. They came as the victor, not the victim. They had a supernatural power which the pagans wanted too.

So every time Christians were martyred, pagans who watched accepted Christ. Thus, Christianity increased and spread until finally it overran the Roman Empire.

One of the Early Church Fathers said, "The blood of the martyrs has become the seed of the church." For when the Christians were persecuted, they fled from Rome out to the ends of the Roman Empire, even into India, and they took with them the message of the Lord Jesus Christ. So Christianity spread over all the then-known world, and the last of those awful despots on his deathbed conceded victory to Christ when he said: "Galilean, thou hast conquered."

So it was that when Constantine came to the throne of Rome, he declared Christianity to be the world religion. Tradition says he marched his armies through the River Tiber and declared them to be Christians. Now you know that is not the way to make Christians. He took the pagan temples where they worshiped all the gods of ancient Rome, closed them one day, opened them the next day and declared them to be Christian churches. Suddenly it became popular to be a Christian. To get a job in the government one had to join the "Christian" party. Thus, the Roman Empire suddenly, by official decree from the Emperor himself, became Christian in name, but not in reality.

3. THE PERGAMOS PERIOD — A.D. 300 - 500

That brings us to the Pergamos period, prophetically from about A.D. 300-500. I am sorry to tell you this period is not a beautiful one. The word "Pergamos" in verse 12 means "married." The world and the church got married and the church suddenly lost its power. In the Smyrna period the church was spiritually powerful because she was pure. When an individual accepted Christ during the time of the Smyrna period, that individual knew that he would probably have to give up everything he had: his property, his friends, his family, possibly his life. He knew that he would probably not live long enough to die a natural death. So he accepted Christ with the thought that he was surrendering himself totally to the Saviour together with all that he possessed. The result was a demonstration of supernatural spiritual power. But when we come to the Pergamos period, we find the world and the church combining and the church lost its power. Suddenly it is popular to belong to the church; there is no more persecution. If anything now, the persecution is going to be against those who don't join the church or against those who still try to be real Biblical Christians. And this happened in due time.

Having visited the site of Pergamos, I would like to explain verse 13. Follow in your Bible:

> I know thy works, and where thou dwellest, even where Satan's seat is: and thou holdest fast my name, and hast not denied my faith, even in those days wherein Antipas was my faithful martyr, who was slain among you, where Satan dwelleth.

The town of Pergamos is located at the base of a hill called a citadel. Many of the Turkish towns are like that. In ancient times they used the citadel for a fortress in case of attack by an enemy. While visiting the citadel of Pergamos I walked on the ground where the guide said they used to worship Satan in ancient times. I think that is where Satan's seat was and my guess is that Antipas was a Christian in the first century, back there in the days of John, who was taken up there and martyred in connection with and in the place where they worshiped the devil.

But now prophetically from A.D. 300-500 we have the condition described in the rest of the verse where we have the doctrine of Balaan and the doctrine of the Nicolaitanes coming into existence. The doctrine of Balaan is engaging in religion for money. The doctrine of the Nicolaitanes involves the clergy lording it over the laity of the church. This is what happened during this period. The church lost its purity and so it lost its spiritual power. And all history was changed!

The throne of the Caesars toppled and fell and the Roman Empire crumbled in the dust. But the bishop of the church of Rome took to himself the opportunity to sit on a throne and expand that throne far beyond the power of the Roman emperors. He called it the Holy Roman Empire. He further claimed to have power to condemn men to eternal hell or into pergatory or to get them out if he chose. Thus, we have the beginning of the papacy. Don't let anybody ever convince you that the Roman Catholic Church started in the first century. It did not. It came into being in this period. A tremendous change had taken place from the days of that wonderful church to which Paul addressed the Book of Romans. In the first century they had a beautiful, powerful, Biblical church in Rome. Read the Book of Romans and see for yourself. But it is altogether different when we get to the Pergamos period—A.D. 300-500. It's a period when the world and the church got married and John told all about it long before it happened.

4. THE THYATIRA PERIOD — A.D. 500 - 1500

That brings us to the fourth period—Thyatira. We are not surprised that the Thyatira church is a very, very disappointing one. Here we cover a period of history from about A.D. 500-1500—roughly a thousand years. Secular history calls this period the Dark Ages. But secular history cannot adequately explain why the Dark Ages came upon the world. You must know the Bible to understand that. Remember this was the time when the church and the world were united. The church had lost its power spiritually. And now the church in the name of Jesus Christ began to put Jews and evangelical Christians to death if they wouldn't join the Roman church. The order came from the throne of the Holy Roman Empire as it was called.

During this period some evangelicals—little groups of them here and there like the Waldenses and Albigenses and others— evangelical Christians trying to hang on to the truth—were persecuted unmercifully by the Church of Rome. This is history. But during this period of roughly a thousand years, the church plunged the world into the Dark Ages. And it all happened because they had forsaken the Bible. They had forsaken the Lord and they began to set up a man-made system in the name of Christ. If you read the story of Jezebel in this chapter, you will have a description of the professing church in the days of the Middle Ages. If you want to know more about this, read *Haley's Bible Handbook,* pages 866 to 881, giving the story of the papacy. Everybody ought to read it.

5. THE SARDIS PERIOD — A.D. 1500 - 1700

We come now to chapter 3 and the fifth period in church history. Here we have the letter addressed to Sardis. Sardis is the church of the remnant. God always has His remnant. During this time men like Zwingly, Huss, Melanchthon, Martin Luther, and others began to examine the Scriptures and publicly proclaim what they found. Martin Luther found that wonderful verse: "the just shall live by faith." As a Roman Catholic priest, he had beaten himself with a whip until he could hardly walk, trying to atone for his sins but he could find no relief. He could find no satisfaction for his soul. Then he found the verse in Galatians and the Holy Spirit led him to see the truth—"the just shall live by faith," not by penance, not by beating oneself, not by climbing the sacred stairs in Rome, but by faith.

Martin Luther had an experience with the Holy Spirit that gave him the courage and the strength and the power to tack his 95 theses to the Wittenburg door. By doing so, he lighted the torch of the reformation fires that was to burn around the world and prophecy became history: The church of Sardis is the church of the remnant, the church of the reformation. In round numbers it covers 200 years from 1500 to 1700. As the people began to study their Bibles, they began to consider living what they were reading. So we have the pietistic movement coming to the fore and that brings us to Philadelphia and number six.

6. THE PHILADELPHIA PERIOD — A.D. 1700 - 1900

This period covers 1700 to 1900 and this is the most beautiful of all. Look at verse 7: "To the angel of the church of Philadelphia . . ."—Philadelphia means "brotherly love." In John's day this city had a great church. Today Philadelphia is a backward, lonely Turkish town. Whenever I read this story I think of the one experience I had there and I want to weep. There are no Christians as far as I can tell in Philadelphia today. And there is no religious liberty to preach about Christ either; I tried it. As tourists, we visited the town of Philadelphia. It lies inland, away from the coast—a nice, clean, little Turkish town surrounded by vineyards.

We asked the guide, "Are there any remains of an ancient Christian church?" He said, "Yes, there are." He took us to see a big pillar, a tremendous post, about 10 feet square and about 20 feet tall, made out of brick. High up on the side was painted a picture of a religious figure. He said, "Tradition says this is a pillar of a fifth-century Christian church." There were houses all around it and I couldn't get a very good picture of it. Right across the street from it was a Moslem mosque. You know those mosques have minarets stretching high up into the sky, from which point the "caller," five times a day, calls the faithful to prayer. The faithful Mohammedans then get down on their knees wherever they are, no matter what they are doing, and kneel toward Mecca and pray. They used to climb the tall minaret to give out the prayer call, but they have gone modern. They now have loud speakers and microphones. They don't need to climb up there anymore.

I asked the guide, "Would it be possible to go up there in the minaret?" I had always wanted to go up in one of those things, but never before could get permission. I told the guide I'd like to go up there to take a picture of that pillar. He inquired and, surprisingly enough, we were granted permission. Four of us climbed this narrow stairway. The whole staircase wasn't much more than two feet wide. It was a spiral. In the center was a post and the stairway spiraled around it, up and up and up. We climbed and climbed and climbed until finally we came out on the balcony way up there. We could see all over the town. It occurred to me that we ought to sing a gospel song. We formed an instant male quartet and sang "Blessed Assurance, Jesus Is Mine." The Mohammedans from all over town looked toward the mosque and wondered what in the world was going on.

When we descended (after taking our pictures, of course), we had an audience. They were coming from all directions. The older people didn't come too close, but the school children jammed in around us. They were beautiful kids with smiling faces. There was a large crowd, as if we were celebrities, just jamming in around us. The street was full of people. There was a wall around the courtyard with a nice ledge on top. I said to our guide, "May I stand up here on the wall and tell these people about Jesus?" I got a quick answer. "Oh no, you can't do that." How sad! Such beautiful children, well fed, friendly, lovely kids but not allowed to hear the story of Christ! That's Philadelphia today.

But in the first century John wrote prophetically picturing the whole of Christianity from 1700 to 1900, by presenting the picture here of Philadelphia. The sixth period of church history was a wonderful period. Look again at verse 7: "These things saith he that is holy, he that is true [notice the description of Christ in view of the condition of the church], he that hath the key of David, he that openeth, and no man shutteth; and shutteth, and no man openeth." This was the church of the open book and the church of the open door. But let me read a little more. "I know thy works; behold, I have set before thee an open door, and no man can shut it; for thou hast a little strength, and hast kept my word, and hast not denied my name."

This was a period of modern missions, not modernistic missions, but modern missions, when a cobbler in his shoemaker's shop in Britain laid down his tools and went off to the Orient to become the "Father of Modern Missions." His name was William Carey. Men like Hudson Taylor and Adoniram Judson, David Livingston, and a host of others went out in a mighty stream to the ends of the earth to take the Gospel to the heathen around the world. Many of them had nobody to sponsor them; they just went out by faith. Many of them suffered severely. Many of them experienced tribulation and much difficulty, but nevertheless, they went. Some of them became martyrs but others replaced them and the Lord says of this church something He doesn't say about any of the others. In a special way, He says: ". . . I have loved thee" (v. 9).

This is the church that proclaimed the Gospel of Jesus Christ. It opened the whole Book, taught men to live by the Book. This is in contrast to the Reformation Period. In the Reformation Period, they had the truth, but they had not yet learned to apply it to their lives. Their lives were not as holy as they should have been. As they studied their Bibles they came to the place where they realized they ought to be more pious, ought to be more holy, ought to live according to what they read. Thus, history calls them Pietists.

The Philadelphia period is the period when this thing came into bloom. During this period all the great Protestant denominations came into existence, breaking away from the old corrupt systems of Catholicism. So we have the Episcopalians, the Presbyterians, the Baptists, the Brethren, the Lutherans, the Methodists, and so on. It is remarkable that all of them, while they did not agree entirely in every detail, and differed in liturgy and forms of worship, nevertheless all of them essentially believed the Bible was the very Word of God. They believed that Jesus was the Son of God, that He was the Saviour, that there was a heaven and a hell. They believed that men were lost without Christ, but in Christ they were saved.

It is said that John Knox preached with such conviction and power that the queen herself "quaked in her boots" when he preached. His followers were called Presbyterians.

The Wesley brothers preached without fear or favor and thousands of Methodist churches were started throughout America and indeed the whole world. Untold thousands accepted Christ as Saviour in old-fashioned Methodist revival meetings. And it all started in the Philadelphia period.

For approximately 200 years, from 1700 to 1900, the missionaries went out to every continent on earth and to the isles of the sea. They proclaimed the unsearchable riches of Christ and millions were ushered into the kingdom of the Lord Jesus Christ. From God's standpoint, it was a great period.

I almost wish I could tell you at this point the Lord came and ended the age of grace. But if He had, you and I would have missed heaven. We weren't even born.

7. THE LAODICEAN PERIOD — 1900 - ?

So we come now to the seventh and last period—the period of Laodicea. It's the twentieth century and it's a sad story. We read in verse 14: "Unto the angel of the church of Laodiceans"—this is the lukewarm church. Now, look, Jesus is getting ready to wind it up. This is the end of the age. "These things saith the Amen" (that is the great Amen), "the faithful and true witnesses, the beginning of the creation of God; I know thy works, that thou art neither cold nor hot: I would thou wert cold or hot. So then because thou art lukewarm, and neither cold nor hot, I will spew thee out of my mouth."

Jesus is saying to the church as a whole at the end of the age, "I am going to repudiate you." This is not surprising when you discover what is happening in Christendom as a whole across this country and around the world. It has become popular now to say that the God of historic Christianity, the God of the Bible, is dead. It has become popular now to say that Jesus is not God; He is just a good man who lived a good life. It has become popular now to deny the miracles of the Bible, to deny the virgin birth, to deny the blood atonement, to deny the bodily resurrection, to deny the bodily ascension, and to deny His bodily return.

And yet those who deny these things don't want to go out of business; they want to have a church. They don't want to be against the Lord and they don't want to be for the Lord. The Lord says, I want you to be either for me or against me; I don't want you to be lukewarm. Either be cold or be hot, one of the two, but don't straddle the fence. Jesus says to this church, "I will spue thee out" (repudiate you). I didn't write it. This is what He says and this is what has happened.

Roughly speaking, we can say with the coming of the twentieth century, the seeds of Laodicean religion were sown. It started in the theological schools of Europe. Then it spread to schools that were founded by godly fundamental, Bible-believing, Christ-exalting Christians. I am talking about Yale, Harvard, Columbia, Princeton and the rest of them. In all of these schools, including the seminaries, men in the name of education began to question the truth of the Bible. They began to question the miracles. They began to doubt the story of creation. And one thing led to another.

First there were only questions and in the name of education, they were examining the evidence they said, but after a while they went beyond questions, and they began to teach boldly that the Bible was not true. With each passing decade their blasphemy and heresy intensified until today the majority of our seminaries, our pastors, and our churches have departed entirely from the basic, fundamental, cardinal, Biblical doctrines of historic Christianity. This is Laodicea, the period of apostasy.

During the twentieth century, slowly but surely, the seeds of apostasy were sown, and they began to sprout here and there until they developed into a plant. And now they are beginning to bear fruit. The apostasy is upon us.

When the theologians of four prominent seminaries of this country are pictured in *Time* magazine, with the caption "God is dead," and their churches do not repudiate them, that is surely a sign of apostasy. Apostasy means turning away from the truth.

I have here a document which comes from the United Church of Christ, the United Presbyterian Church, and the United Evangelical Church. Now don't get mad at me for saying this. It is right here and I didn't write it. The document is prepared for young people in the colleges of our land. I wouldn't dare read it to you; it is too pornographic. It is a four-page paper giving, in detail, the experience that young people ought to have in what we call "free love." And this is published in the name of those three churches and being freely distributed among the college students of the country.

I can't understand why the people who are paying to have that printed don't rise up in rebellion and throw out the leaders who would print such trash, such filth. The whole idea is that the old morality is out and now the new world which they are trying to build is a world of free love. They say it will take a while before everybody will be sympathetic to this kind of thing, but we can't wait—that is what it says, "We can't wait, we've got to move out now." They say they are building a brand-new world where we will not have marriages that have vows. They would do away with the marriage vows. Oh, we will have marriages, but it is just for the convenience of two people living together to raise a family. Free love is the order of it. It makes you sick to read it! Now, if it were written by the smut peddlers, you would expect that. But when it comes in the name of Christian churches, what in the world are we coming to? I am trying to tell you what God says is going to happen and I am utterly amazed that:

IT IS HAPPENING — NOW!

Yes, the Laodicean church is the church of the apostasy. And I am reminded that Paul said in chapter 2 of his second letter to the Thessalonians that the coming of the Lord would be preceded by a period of falling away. And that "falling away" is apostasy. It is the Greek word *apostasia* from which we get the English word "apostasy." The period of apostasy must also precede the appearance of the Antichrist. We are in that period of apostasy now. All of the major denominations of America were at one time more or less fundamental. But there is now one left that has not started down the road of apostasy and history will show that there is no cure for apostasy but judgment.

It is now a matter of "calling out a people for His name." At the end of this age, I am sorry to tell you, we will not have a great worldwide revival where everybody will be coming to Christ. There will be a great moving of the Holy Spirit and many will be saved. We see that in many areas. But basically, it will be a matter of snatching a few here and there. As the world gets worse and worse the Lord is purifying a people for His name. He is getting ready to take the Bride up. But in the meantime, many churches are heading down the broad road of apostasy. They will join the world on the broad road that leads to hell.

Jesus said (v. 17):

Because thou sayest, I am rich, and increased in goods, and have need of nothing; and knowest not that thou art wretched, and miserable, and poor, and blind, and naked: I counsel thee to buy of me gold tried in the fire, that thou mayest be rich; and white raiment, that thou mayest be clothed, and that the shame of thy nakedness do not appear; and anoint thine eyes with eyesalve, that thou mayest see. As many as I love, I rebuke and chasten: be zealous therefore, and repent. BEHOLD, I STAND AT THE DOOR AND KNOCK: . . . .

This is what Jesus says. When this age comes to a close, Christ will be outside the main body of professing Christendom—knocking at the door pleading for admittance.

Jesus promised that where two or three were gathered together in His name, there He would be in their midst. But when a congregation has gathered and they deny the Christ of the Bible, the Lord is not going to be present. He will be outside the door waiting for an invitation to come in. I don't think this period can last much longer.

PREPARE FOR "TAKE-OFF" — SOON!

Before the apostate world-church is finally complete, the true believers will have to leave. When we leave, this age will have ended. This is exciting. We are going up! How soon? I don't know. But I look for it any time.

Thus, we finally come to the end of this age of grace, this present church age, and this period in the Book of Revelation with these words:

> BEHOLD, I STAND AT THE DOOR, AND KNOCK: AND IF ANY MAN [now it is an individual invitation] HEAR MY VOICE, AND OPEN THE DOOR [that is the door of his heart], I WILL COME IN TO HIM, AND WILL SUP WITH HIM, AND HE WITH ME. To him that overcometh will I grant to sit with me in my throne, even as I also overcame, and am set down with my Father in his throne. He that hath an ear, let him hear . . . .

Did you hear that? Some people don't want to hear this. They don't see it; they don't want to see it. Only those who are open to the truth will see it.

"He that hath an ear, let him hear what the Spirit saith unto the churches." And so the age of grace ends. There is no more! The seventh period will complete the whole. We can see what Christians in no age before us could see, and we know that the end of the age is near. Christ is coming soon!

John wrote seven letters addressing seven historic churches. But in so doing he also wrote a book of prophecy. Yet he did it in such a way that he did not destroy the precious doctrine of the imminent return of Christ. God wanted His children in every age to be constantly looking and watching for His return. The Bible calls it the *Blessed Hope*.

So John did not destroy this doctrine by telling in advance exactly what he was doing. Maybe he didn't know himself. But the Lord knew and He told John to write it in a book. John did just that and now we can look back from our vantage point in time and we can see what could not clearly be seen at any prior point in history. We can see that we have come through six distinct periods of church history as John described them in prophecy and we are now in the seventh and last one. How close we must be to that climactic event when the Lord Himself will appear in the sky for those who love Him.

In our next message, when we start chapter 4, we will be in heaven. I hope you will be here to listen to God's message. Bring your Bible. Bring your friends and your enemies.

Maybe there is somebody here tonight who is unsaved. If you would like to get your name in the Lamb's Book of Life before it is too late, just tell the Lord about it. Tell Him you want to be saved and ask Him to come into your heart. He is waiting, but you must open the door.

LET US PRAY

Our Heavenly Father, we thank Thee tonight for Thy Word. We praise Thee for the Holy Spirit who makes these things plain to all those who search for the truth, but O God, we pray there may be none here tonight who will turn away from the truth, rejecting that which is clearly evident, rejecting the voice of the Holy Spirit, refusing to see that which the Spirit would show them, refusing to hear that which the Spirit would say.

We pray instead that our hearts may be in tune to the still small voice. May we discern His voice and act accordingly. Then we know that Thou wilt bless. But O, our hearts go out to those who, perhaps, in all sincerity, are in the wrong place. We pray that somehow the truth may reach them and that they may "come out from among them and be ye separate," as the Scripture says.

Tonight we praise Thee for the privilege of gathering here to study Thy Word, and for the privilege of listening to the voice of the Holy Spirit as He speaks to our hearts and shows us the deep things of God. We pray that the land of America may yet remain free for a long time. Nevertheless we see the shadows falling on every hand, and we believe it will not be long until we will no longer have the liberty to proclaim the Gospel as we do tonight. So we pray that we may realize the lateness of the hour, the gravity of the situation, the seriousness of the condition.

We pray that each of us may act accordingly and that we may be busy about our Father's business while there is yet time. We pray that Thou shalt rule and overrule from Thy throne in heaven so that the word of the Lord shall go forth and as many as possible may yet be saved before it is too late.

We thank Thee for every blessing from Thy loving hand, not the least of which is the blessing of the indwelling Holy Spirit in the heart of every believer. Make these things plain to every heart. And may all glory and honor and praise be Thine alone. We pray it in Jesus' name. Amen.

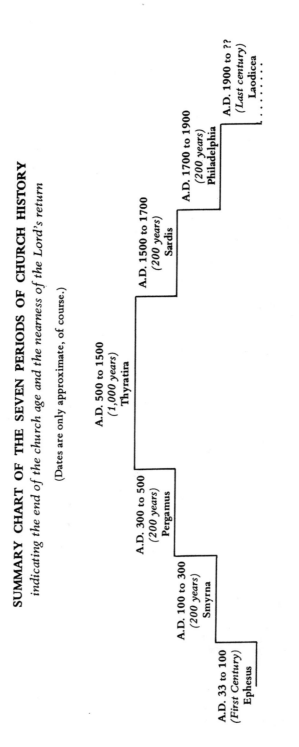

SUMMARY CHART OF THE SEVEN PERIODS OF CHURCH HISTORY

indicating the end of the church age and the nearness of the Lord's return

(Dates are only approximate, of course.)

A.D. 33 to 100
(*First Century*)
Ephesus

A.D. 100 to 300
(*200 years*)
Smyrna

A.D. 300 to 500
(*200 years*)
Pergamus

A.D. 500 to 1500
(*1,000 years*)
Thyratira

A.D. 1500 to 1700
(*200 years*)
Sardis

A.D. 1700 to 1900
(*200 years*)
Philadelphia

A.D. 1900 to ??
(*Last century*)
Laodicea

Part Three

The Things Which
Shall Be Hereafter

III

The Church
in Heaven

REVELATION 4 and 5

We are ready now to go to heaven—in the spirit, of course. We begin the fourth chapter of the Book of Revelation with the words, "After this . . . ." So we stop to ask, "After what?" The answer is found in the previous chapters which contain descriptions of the seven periods of church history covering the age of the church, or the age of grace.

John is saying, "After the church age is over . . . ." So let us continue now:

> After this I looked, and, behold, a door was opened in heaven: and the first voice which I heard was as it were of a trumpet talking with me: which said, Come up hither, and I will shew thee things which must be hereafter.
> And immediately I was in the spirit . . . .

THE OPEN DOOR OF HEAVEN

Notice the things that John mentions here: the open door of heaven, the voice, the trumpet, and the invitation to "come up. . . ." These are the same things mentioned by Paul when he speaks of the Lord coming for His church in I Thessalonians 4:16-17.

> For the Lord himself shall descend from heaven with a shout, with the voice of the archangel, and with the trump of God: and the dead in Christ shall rise first:
> Then we which are alive and remain shall be caught up together with them in the clouds, to meet the Lord in the air: and so shall we ever be with the Lord.

So in each of these accounts we have the rapture of the church. The shout of command coming from the Commander-in-Chief is for all saved ones to rise. The trumpet is God's way of heralding this tremendous event when the bride of His Son is being evacuated out of this old, sin-cursed, war-torn world. She will be transformed and translated into glorified, heavenly creatures fit to be wed to the Son of God Himself.

Notice, too, that it all happens "immediately." There is nothing here about taking a few million years of the evolutionary process for the body to adapt itself to the new environment of space. No indeed! John says "immediately."

Paul told the Corinthian Christians it will happen "in the

twinkling of an eye." Imagine that! Instantly we'll be caught away upward to meet the Lord in the air. In glorified bodies we'll zoom through space with the speed of thought (not light, that's too slow). We'll cover more than ten billion light years of space in a moment of time as we move to the celestial city of God. We'll pass through the portals of pearl and walk down the streets that are made of pure gold. This is the rapture of the church.

Thus, it becomes apparent that we are now in Part III of the outline Jesus gave to John in chapter 1, verse 19:

"THINGS WHICH SHALL BE HEREAFTER"

So from here on, in the Book of Revelation John is dealing with the future—after the Church Age is over. Do not look for the church on earth during the tribulation which begins in chapter 6. She will not be there. She goes to heaven at the beginning of chapter 4. Except on occasions when John uses the journalistic technique of flashback, he writes his story in chronological order—telling things as they happen in time sequence.

Notice next in verses 2 and 3:

THE OCCUPIED THRONE

And immediately I was in the spirit: and, behold, a throne was set in heaven, and one sat on the throne.

And he that sat was to look upon like a jasper and a sardine stone: and there was a rainbow round about the throne, in sight like unto an emerald.

John tells us that he saw a throne in heaven. It was the throne of God—the eternal, omnipotent God, who made the whole universe including every star and every rose.

That throne must be a dazzling spectacle of splendor paling into insignificance such puny thrones as the golden throne of King Tut of Egypt or the Sultan's throne with a mere 15,000 emeralds and 25,000 pearls. The most fabulous thrones of earth's richest monarchs are like dirt when compared with the throne of the King of kings, the Almighty Himself. What a throne!

Magnificent and majestic as the throne may be, however, John's attention is riveted on the One who occupies the throne. For unlike the empty thrones of the Pharaohs and the sultans, the throne of heaven is occupied.

Seated there in all His glory, majesty and power is the One who is "all together lovely." It is Christ Himself soon to be crowned King of kings and Lord of lords. We will worship and adore Him and as we gaze on His face we will realize that He is the very essence of beauty. No thing and no one in all the universe can compare. He is the "Lily of the Valley, the Bright and Morning Star, He's the fairest of ten thousand to my soul."

But notice John has a problem. As he attempts to describe this One who occupies the throne, he is at a loss for words. The reason is simple. There are no words in the original Greek nor in the English which we are using now, to adequately describe such heavenly beauty. Indeed no earthly tongue can tell nor can mortal mind conceive the wonder of it all.

So John must resort to figures of speech. He will use this technique again and again when describing the heavenly realm. After all, Paul wrote:

> . . . Eye hath not seen, nor ear heard, neither have entered into the heart of man, the things which God hath prepared for them that love him (I Cor. 2:9).

So how can John describe this most beautiful of all heavenly beings? He must resort to using figures of speech referring to jewels. Of course, don't forget the Holy Spirit can allow us to catch a faint glimpse of all this glory as Paul suggests: "But God hath revealed them unto us by his spirit . . ." (I Cor. 2:10).

Now look at:

THE RAINBOW — A HEAVENLY HALO

It says there was a rainbow round about the throne, in sight like unto an emerald. Once again he refers to jewels. He will do that many times throughout this book.

Jesus Christ, the one who is altogether lovely, the Lord of lords, the King of kings, His Majesty, the omnipotent God is seated on the throne of heaven and around His head is the most beautiful rainbow you have ever seen.

But let's stop for a moment to ask the question, "What is the significance of the rainbow?"

I have a special appreciation for rainbows. When I was preaching for the missionaries in Hawaii, the Lord put a few rainbows, and I mean a few, out there in the sky every morning. Hawaii, to me, is the land of rainbows. We looked out over Pearl Harbor and there, touching the beautiful Pacific, was a rainbow arching the sky with the other end anchored on the mountain ridge. And then just for good measure, the Lord put another one right over it. From the sea to the mountain every morning, and sometimes during the day—lovely, lovely rainbows!

So what is the significance of the rainbows? Remember the first rainbow. When God brought Noah out of the ark after the flood was over, God put a rainbow in the heavens. For the first time, men saw a rainbow. It was a testimonial to the faithfulness of God to keep His promise. Mankind would never again be destroyed with a flood.

When we get to heaven and look upon the One who made all this possible, we shall see a rainbow as a halo 'round His head and we shall realize that God keeps His word. The storms of life are past. God is on the throne, and all is well.

TWENTY-FOUR THRONES

Verse 4:

And round about the throne were four and twenty seats: and upon the seats I saw four and twenty elders sitting, clothed in white raiment; and they had on their heads crowns of gold.

The word "seats" indicates the seat of a king, so we really have 24 thrones occupied by the "elders."

We must stop to ask the question, "Who are the elders?" And when I tell you the answer you'll want to know, "Why didn't God say so in simple words?"

The answer is: this is a love letter that God is writing to His children. It is written so that those who love Him enough to study the Word will find the answers to many questions in various parts of the Bible. Thus, the whole of God's revealed Word will begin to unfold and it will have meaning. Those who are simply interested out of curiosity, so that they can argue with God's Word and make fun of God's children, may read it and not know what it is all about. This is an open love letter, but it has a private message. If you are a Bible reader, you will know right away, that in the Old Testament, God speaks of elders in relation to the Old Testament saints, the elders of Israel. You will know also that in the New Testament the church had elders. So you see, there is a relationship here to saved ones. The devil never has elders.

Next question: why 24? Answer: First of all, it is symbolic. Very soon when these elders begin to sing they indicate that they are redeemed ones from the planet Earth. And John says that they number 10,000 times 10,000 and many more beyond that. So it is obvious that the number 24 is symbolic.

But why 24? Maybe we have a clue in I Chronicles 24 where David divided the Levitical priesthood into 24 groups or courses. Each group elected representatives to go up to the temple and conduct the services of the temple. So that when a group had served in the temple by representation, it was credited to them all as if they had all served. Thus, the Levitical priesthood was divided by David into 24 courses. Can it be that God is here telling us that He is dividing the Heavenly priesthood into 24 courses?

At any rate, by the time we get through with the next chapter, I think there can be no doubt about who the elders are. They represent the redeemed ones for they sing the song of redemption ending with the words in chapter 5, verse 10: "and hast made us unto our God kings and priests. . . ." Furthermore, this explanation fits into the context better than any other explanation that you can possibly make.

First of all, they are seated on thrones and that is in keeping with the Biblical teaching. They are clothed in white raiment. That is exactly how we will be clothed (see chap. 19, v. 8). And they have on their heads crowns of gold. At the end of this chapter, we shall discover what they do with those crowns. But now let us look at verse 5.

And out of the throne proceeded lightnings and thunderings and voices: and there were seven lamps of fire burning before the throne, which are the seven Spirits of God.

Here we have seven spiritual beings—that is, angels. We shall meet them again in future chapters. Remember, there is only one Holy Spirit and He is a member of the Trinity, one of the persons of the Godhead. But these who are here called the seven spirits of God, according to references which we will come to later, are angelic beings, who do the bidding of God. They are waiting in the wing, so to speak, ready to do what God wants done, like blowing the seven trumpets, pouring out the seven last plagues, and so forth.

FOUR LIVING CREATURES

We are ready now for verse 6:

And before the throne there was a sea of glass like unto crystal: and in the midst of the throne, and round about the throne, were four beasts full of eyes before and behind.

The word "beast" in the King James English of 1611 is archaic now. The more literal translation would be "living creatures." So I shall read it that way from now on whenever I come to it in this book. We will meet them again a number of times. There are four special angelic beings, living creatures, standing around the throne of God as an honor guard. These four living creatures are full of eyes, before and behind. They can see in all directions at one time.

And the first beast was like a lion, and the second beast like a calf, and the third beast had a face as a man, and the fourth beast was like a flying eagle.

In their very appearance, they suggest the attributes of God. The first living creature was like a lion, suggesting the kingship of God. The second living creature was like a calf (the Greek says an ox) suggesting service. The Bible says when we get to heaven, the Lord Jesus is going to serve us. I can't understand that, but that is what it says. The third living creature had a face like a man—that can speak of only one thing—intelligence. The face of a man is unique above all else in God's creation, and it indicates intelligence. Our God is an intelligent God. And the fourth living creature was like a flying eagle. That suggests majesty, mobility, power of sight, and so forth. But all of these things in some way seem to suggest some of the attributes of our God.

Now verse 8 says:

> And the four beasts had each of them six wings about him; and they were full of eyes within: and they rest not day and night, saying, Holy, holy, holy, Lord God Almighty, which was and is, and is to come.

These living creatures display the attributes of God as they stand as an honor guard about the throne of God, but they also chant His holiness. And as these beautiful heavenly creatures chant "Holy, holy, holy," do you know what we will do? We, as redeemed mortals from the planet Earth, newcomers to the celestial city, will watch and listen: then we'll fall on our faces to worship Him that sits upon the throne and we'll lay our crowns at His feet ascribing all worthiness, honor, glory, and praise to Him alone. Verses 9, 10 and 11 tell us so.

> And when those beasts give glory and honour and thanks to him that sat on the throne, who liveth for ever and ever,
> The four and twenty elders fall down before him that sat on the throne, and worship him that liveth for ever and ever, and cast their crowns before the throne, saying, Thou art worthy, O Lord, to receive glory and honour and power: for thou hast created all things, and for thy pleasure they are and were created.

CROWNS OF REWARD

He will place crowns of reward on our heads. But when we see all the splendor of heaven, all the glory of His person, we will realize as we never realized before that "Jesus paid it all, all to Him I owe. Sin had left a crimson stain; He washed it white as snow." In a spontaneous outburst of adoration and praise we are going to prostrate ourselves before Him in worship. We will take the crowns off our heads and lay them at His feet. Then we will say, "Thou art worthy, O Lord, to receive glory and honour and power: for thou hast created all things, for thy pleasure they are and were created."

Every person here tonight was made for a purpose. A woman once said to me, "I don't know why I was ever born." Well, here's the answer. You were made to give God pleasure.

How can we best give God pleasure? To get the answer we must consider what the Bible teaches about our relation to Him as bride and groom. The New Testament church is called the bride—His bride whom He loves very dearly.

So how does a bride give her husband pleasure? By working? No! No! He could hire a scrub woman for that. She gives him pleasure when she says to him, "I love you!"

Now when God's children spontaneously overflow in loving adoration and praise to their redeemer, that's worship! Worship is for God alone and it is the highest form of pleasure finite beings can give to their creator and Lord.

Some children give their earthly parents nothing but heartache and tears. Some earthly children give their parents great pleasure. So some of God's children give their Heavenly Father nothing but grief. Then, too, some of His children give Him a great deal of pleasure.

Now we are ready for chapter 5 and that tremendous scene which we call:

THE CORONATION OF THE KING OF KINGS

It all starts with the Father seated on the throne and the Son likewise seated with Him. The Father is holding in His hand a scroll, that is called a little book. We shall see later that this is really the title deed of the planet Earth.

Suddenly an angel breaks the heavenly silence by shouting to all the assembled hosts of heaven: "Who is worthy to open the book?"

John explains how he looked all over the hosts of heaven for one to respond. But among all the redeemed mortals and among all the holy angels, there was not a single one who answered the call. Then John looked to the only other possible place in the universe—the planet Earth. He looked all around the earth on its surface where the "living" mortals dwell. There was no response. So he exhausted the possibilities by looking into the heart of the earth where the lost of all ages in Hades await the final judgment. Alas! There was no response from any area and John tells us he began to weep. So important was the invitation.

But one of the heavenly beings told John to turn around and look toward the throne. Evidently in his diligent search he had turned his back to the throne, so he had to be told where the action was. Now read it for yourself so you'll know I didn't make it up. Chapter 5, verses 1 through 4:

> And I saw in the right hand of him that sat on the throne a book written within and on the backside, sealed with seven seals.
>
> And I saw a strong angel proclaiming with a loud voice, Who is worthy to open the book, and to loose the seals thereof?
>
> And no man in heaven, nor in earth, neither under the earth, was able to open the book, neither to look thereon.
>
> And I wept much, because no man was found worthy to open and to read the book, neither to look thereon.

Now see also verses 5 and 6:

> And one of the elders saith unto me, Weep not: behold the Lion of the tribe of Juda, the Root of David, hath prevailed to open the book, and to loose the seven seals thereof.
>
> And I beheld, and, lo, in the midst of the throne, and of the four beasts, and in the midst of the elders, stood a Lamb as it had been slain, having seven horns and seven eyes, which are the seven Spirits of God sent forth into all the earth.

THE LION

So John looks toward the throne and he sees One responding. He is called a lion, specifically "The Lion of the tribe of Juda." And what Bible student does not know that this is Christ?

Then notice too, John sees

THE LAMB

And where is it? In the throne surrounded by the elders and the four living creatures. Notice also that it is the lamb that was slain. Every Bible student knows that John the Baptist, pointing to Christ, said, ". . . Behold the Lamb of God, which taketh away the sin of the world" (John 1:29).

So the lion and the lamb are one and the same, namely, Christ. But what's all this got to do with the coronation? Everything!

According to Jeremiah 32 the Old Testament method of securing a property required: (1) He had to be heir to the property—that is, he had to be in the line of inheritance; (2) He had to have the money to pay the purchase price. Jeremiah fulfilled both of these requirements (see Jer. 32:8-10). So after he had laid down the money, he was given the title deed in the form of a scroll. Then in the presence of the town fathers he broke the seals and opened it. Thus, he had "recorded his deed in the court house."

Thus, we find in Jeremiah 32 the key that unlocks Revelation 5. As the Lion, Christ shows He is heir to the throne; He is the King. Remember, it was prophesied at His birth: ". . . and the Lord God shall give unto him the throne of his father David . . . and of his kingdom there shall be no end" (Luke 1:32-33).

Then, too, as the Lamb, He indicates that He is the one who paid the purchase price, namely, His own blood. John the Baptist identified Him in John 1:29 by saying, ". . . Behold the Lamb of God, which taketh away the sin of the world."

So the coronation ceremony gets underway. The Father holds up the little book (the scroll which is the title deed of earth) and the angel gives the call: "Who is worthy to open the book?" Then Christ, the Lion-Lamb, stands up, ready to take the book. All heaven is filled with admiration and awe.

Notice the reference to the seven Spirits in verse 6. This is the same special group of angelic beings we talked about in the fifth verse of the previous chapter. They are ready to go into action. What a momentous occasion! The only one in the universe who has the right to be crowned King of kings and Lord of lords will now be thus exalted. And the hosts of heaven are ready.

In verses 7 and 8 we read:

And he came and took the book out of the right hand of him that sat upon the throne.

And when he had taken the book, the four beasts and four and twenty elders fell down before the Lamb, having every one of them harps, and golden vials full of odours, which are the prayers of saints.

Christ the Lion-Lamb declares Himself heir and purchaser. Then He takes the book, ready to break the seals. When the book is finally open He will be declared King and owner. He, whose right it is to reign, will reign over His property—namely, the planet Earth.

But notice now

THE HARP ORCHESTRA

As angels and redeemed mortals prostrate themselves in adoration and worship before His Majesty, the elders (that's us) begin to play on their heavenly harps. I'm so glad John specifically records that "every one" has a harp. When the musical talent was handed out, I didn't get too much. And if the record here said that everybody except one had a harp, I'd know who was left out. So I'm glad it says, "having every one of them harps."

Can you imagine how that will sound, when all together in flawless rendition, we'll all play on our heavenly harps the praises of our redeemer.

And notice something else. When we begin to play, the halls of heaven will be filled with a fragrance that is divine.

PRAYERS CHANGE INTO PERFUME

John tells us that God has accumulated the prayers of his saints over the centuries and stored them in golden bowls for this special occasion. When we touch the strings of those golden harps, the atmosphere of heaven will be permeated with an aroma that will delight us beyond words.

Some people think their prayers are oftimes lost somewhere between earth and heaven, but now we know that every sincere prayer directed to God through Christ reaches the throne room of heaven. And regardless of what answer we may observe, God is holding those prayers stored up in golden bowls for a special purpose at the coronation ceremony.

Personally, I hope the perfume is jasmine. The jasmine flowers of Egypt are positively exotic. Egypt has its share of unpleasant smells, but whenever I visit the land of the Pharaohs, I look for a ragged little boy selling jasmine flowers strung up like a pearl necklace. My wife calls me Ferdinand because I enjoy smelling flowers—and jasmine is my favorite. Well, whatever it is, I'm sure the perfume of heaven will exceed our wildest imagination. And it's just one of the many pleasures the Lord has in store for us in heaven.

Let me tell this story to encourage you. I was preaching in Dayton, Ohio. I gave the invitation after the message and an old man came down the aisle. I did not know how old he was, but in talking to him afterward, I found out he was 83 years old. That was the oldest man I had ever seen come to Christ in any of the services where I was preaching. Prior to that time, the oldest man I had ever had a part in helping lead to the Lord was 80 years old. Since then, a man 90 years old was saved in a church in the beautiful hills of Pennsylvania. But this man was 83.

He didn't tell me the most beautiful part of the story. He was definitely saved. I'm sure of that. But the best part of the story came later when the pastor said: "That man's sister passed away a few years ago at the age of 82 after having prayed all her life for the salvation of her lost brother." She was in heaven before she knew her brother was saved. Her brother, at the age of 83, walked down the aisle and took Jesus Christ as his Saviour.

Now, if you have prayed only a year or two, or ten or twenty—don't give up, not at least for 82 years. I suppose the Lord Himself would not blame you if you stopped then, but at least pray that long. And be reminded of the fact that God hears.

I don't know all about how God answers prayer. All I know is that He wants us to pray, and I do know He does answer prayer. There is not a Christian here who has been a Christian any length of time but what you know that is true. And most of you could give tremendous testimonies about how God has performed miracles for you.

Many of you here in the audience prayed for my wife when I was in this area last February. I asked at the Bible conference that everybody should pray. I was going home to take my wife to the hospital. The doctor thought she had cancer and ordered an operation. When the doctor came out of the operating room, he looked at me and said, "I can find nothing."

I said, "Praise the Lord."

Then he said, "But we are testing some more tissue and after a few days we will know more." Well, after three or four days, the answer was still the same. So I take it the Lord answered prayer, and we thank Him for it. And I thank you for your prayers.

Now, if God doesn't seem to answer your prayer in the way that you think He ought, just be patient, continue to trust Him. Remember, the prayers are stored up there. When we get there, they will serve as perfume at the coronation ceremony of the King of kings. So keep on praying: "Thy will be done; Thy kingdom come." It is coming! And this is the coronation ceremony we are talking about. The Lord is getting ready to break the seals, and we are going into action.

And that brings us to the next item on the agenda of the coronation ceremony and I think this is the best of all so far!

THE HEAVENLY CHOIR

We cannot find words to express how thrilling it will be to sing in that mighty choir when the blood-washed throng bursts forth spontaneously in rapturous tones of love, giving all honor, glory, and praise to the One who redeemed them with His blood and made possible all the ecstasy of heaven which they are now enjoying. Listen for the music and let the Holy Spirit allow you to catch a glimpse of that glory as you read the words of the song in verses 9 and 10:

> And they sung a new song, saying, Thou art worthy to take the book, and to open the seals thereof: for thou wast slain, and hast

redeemed us to God by the blood out of every kindred, and tongue, and people, and nation;

And hast made us unto our God kings and priests: and we shall reign on the earth.

Did you notice we'll be singing about the blood. Some people say: "We don't want a slaughter-house religion," and, consequently, they cut out of the hymnals the songs about the blood. What a tragedy! For without the shedding of blood, there is no remission of sins (Heb. 9:22). Don't you see, friends, it is the blood of Christ, shed on the cross for us, that makes our redemption possible.

The blood of God's Son is the most priceless commodity in the universe. There is absolutely nothing that can get a man to heaven apart from the blood of the Crucified One. So let me tell you: if you refuse to sing about the blood here below, you'll never be present to sing in the heavenly choir.

I was thrilled, while attending the Baptist Church in Moscow, to hear that wonderful choir sing (in Russian, of course): "There is a fountain filled with blood, Drawn from Immanuel's veins, And sinners, plunged beneath that flood, Lose all their guilty stains."

Notice, also, people will be there from every kindred, language, people and nation. This is no problem here inasmuch as innocent children are automatically saved. Since children of every group of mortals die, heaven will surely have some from every earthly tribe even if the missionaries did not yet reach them at the time of the rapture. (Note: Matt. 24:14 refers to the tribulation period, not this present church age. The Lord's coming will not necessarily wait until everybody has heard. Read Rev. 14:6 and see how Matt. 24:14 is fulfilled during the tribulation after the Christians have gone to heaven.)

Now look at verse 10 where John tells us that we shall reign on the earth. We are already in heaven singing. But we are going back to reign. As we move on through this book, we'll see how this all comes to pass.

Well, there you have the words of the song which angels

cannot sing. This is the song of redemption which only mortals, redeemed from the earth, can sing. Remember, if you love the Lord, you'll be in that choir and how thrilling it will be.

Read verses 11 and 12:

> And I beheld, and I heard the voice of many angels round about the throne and the beasts and the elders: and the number of them was ten thousand times ten thousand, and thousands of thousands;
>
> Saying with a loud voice, Worthy is the Lamb that was slain to receive power, and riches, and wisdom, and strength, and honour, and glory, and blessing.

The voice of the angels is heard along with a hundred million elders plus thousands of thousands more. Ten thousand times ten thousand is one hundred million. And a thousand times a thousand is a million. So John says there are many millions more than a hundred million. Imagine that! All in one choir.

Now surely the angels cannot sing the song of the redeemed which only the elders sing in verse 9. So I imagine there is a kind of heavenly antiphonal arrangement when the elders sing and the angels respond in a chant giving all honor to the King as is indicated in verse 12.

Try to imagine what it will be like with a mighty choir of more than a hundred million voices, all spontaneously pouring forth music in perfect pitch and harmony, and all singing the praises of our God. Oh, how we'll make the courts of heaven ring!

And just think, you'll never need to take a voice lesson. Who ever heard of a canary taking a singing lesson? The songbird feels happy. So he puts back his little head, his throat begins to vibrate and then he lets it flow. Out comes a beautiful song. The God who notes the sparrow's fall will certainly do no less for us.

And while we are singing the praises of our Saviour in that great choir, we will suddenly realize that

UNIVERSAL ADORATION

and praise are pouring in from all over God's creation. The fish in the sea, the rocks in the hills, the trees in the forests, the stars in the sky—all are blending their voices in praise to their creator.

Man lowered a microphone into the briny deep and listened

to the fish. To us it's static, to God it's music. Then the scientists made a radio telescope big as a football field. They aimed it on a star and suddenly there was great excitement. For a moment they thought they had contacted intelligent life in space. They were getting a rhythmic pattern from a far-off star. They turned it to another and another. Each star was giving off vibrations. To man it's static, to God it's music. Now we know that everything God has made is giving off vibrations.

Think what it will be like when that great choir begins to sing and all that God has made bursts forth like a mighty "organ of the universe," like the "symphony of the spheres"—all furnishing background music accompanying the redeemed saints in praise to our God.

Read it for yourself, so you know I didn't make it up. Verses 13 and 14:

> And every creature which is in heaven, and on the earth, and under the earth, and such as are in the sea, and all that are in them, heard I saying, Blessing and honour, and glory, and power, be unto him that sitteth upon the throne, and unto the Lamb for ever and ever.
> And the four beasts said, Amen. And the four and twenty elders fell down and worshipped him that liveth for ever and ever.

As we finish singing, those four special angels around the throne say, Amen! That means: "so be it, Lord!" And we will at that point all fall down before Him to lovingly worship the one who alone is worthy. Oh, how we will love Him!

And so we end the scene on our faces before the Lion-Lamb who holds the title deed—ready to break the first seal. When all the seals are broken, He will be declared King of kings. And in due time He (and we with Him) will return to reign on the earth.

In the next chapter we'll see the devil go into action setting up a temporary phony king—the Antichrist.

Meanwhile, don't fail to answer the invitation to sing in that heavenly choir. The invitation is out now: Whosoever will . . . . But you must give an answer. If you are not saved at this point, ask Jesus to come into your heart and He will save you. He loves you; He died for you; He prepared heaven for you. How can you turn Him down?

LET US PRAY

Our Heavenly Father, we praise Thee for the Word of God. We thank Thee for the Holy Spirit who delights to take the deep things of God and make them plain so all can understand. We thank Thee for the assurance that we have that the Holy Spirit dwells within the hearts of all believers. We thank Thee that even though "eye hath not seen, nor ear heard, neither have entered into the heart of man, the things which God hath prepared for them that love him," yet Thou hast revealed them to us by Thy Spirit, and we thank Thee that we have seen what the Spirit has to offer us in the glory world. We rejoice and we long for the day when we shall rise to meet our Saviour in the air and all these experiences shall be ours.

Lord, make us all so homesick for heaven that we will tire of this old world. At the same time, help us to realize we have an assignment. We are ambassadors for Thee in a foreign land. Help us not to get our roots too deep into this world, but help us to realize that our home is in heaven. Our citizenship is beyond the stars, and very soon now, our Saviour and our King is coming to take us to meet Him and we must give a report of what we have done.

So help us each who names the name of Christ to be faithful so that we can give a satisfactory report. We want to hear the words "Well done, thou good and faithful servant" coming from the lips of our Saviour. We thank Thee, Lord, that even though in our own strength we can do nothing, yet in the Holy Spirit wonderful things can be accomplished. So we give Thee all the praise.

Then we pray for any here who may be unsaved. May the Holy Spirit minister to them and bring them to Thyself before it's too late. Help them to see the glory that can be theirs in heaven. Help them to see that the burden of sin will be removed and the doubts shall roll away if only they will submit themselves to the Saviour and acknowledge Him as Lord.

Our Heavenly Father, we pray that the message tonight may ring long in the hearts of those who have heard and that we shall constantly love Thee more and serve Thee better, always looking for the day when He shall return. Meanwhile, help us to be faithful, working even as we are watching.

So finish the message in every heart and may it all be for our good and for Thy glory. We pray it in the matchless name that is above every name, even the name of Jesus. Amen.

IV

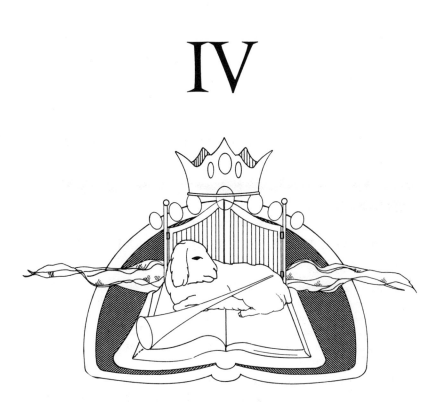

The Coming World Ruler

REVELATION 6 through 13

Jean Dixon says that he is alive right now, that he was born on February 5, 1962, and before this century is out, he will rule the world. She might be right, but so far she has been right only about half of the time. That's not good enough for preaching. So I'll preach from the Book that has been right 100 percent of the time, as we talk about

THE ANTICHRIST – THE COMING WORLD RULER

Open your Bibles to chapter 6 and let us begin our study of the man who will rule the world after the true believers have gone to heaven.

THE FIRST SEAL
AND THE WHITE HORSE OF THE ANTICHRIST

Verses 1 and 2:

And I saw when the Lamb opened one of the seals, and I heard, as it were the noise of thunder, one of the four beasts [living creatures] saying, Come and see.

And I saw, and behold a white horse: and he that sat on him had a bow; and a crown was given unto him: and he went forth conquering and to conquer.

When this action starts on earth, the Lamb is in heaven at the coronation ceremony. The Lamb is the Lord and He is holding the little book, the title deed of earth, in His hand. As He breaks the first seal, the rider on the white horse makes his appearance on the earth below. Therefore, the rider cannot be the true Christ. However, he comes in imitation of the true Christ. In chapter 19 we shall see that Christ comes riding out of heaven in mighty power on a white horse when He comes to reign as King of kings and Lord of lords.

So here we have His imitator coming on a white horse. He is the Wicked One, the Lawless One, the Son of Perdition. He comes as a man but he is the devil's Christ; that is,' the Antichrist. Later in this book John calls him "the beast." He is the first of the four horsemen of the Apocalypse. Don't let that word frighten you. Apocalypse is the Greek word for Revelation; it means "to reveal or unveil."

This beast will rule the world with satanic power and will

demand that everyone worship him as God. We will see the Scripture for that later, but here we are told he goes forth conquering. He promises peace but brings war—indeed the most awful war the world has ever seen. That brings us to

THE SECOND SEAL AND THE RED HORSE OF WAR

Verses 3 and 4:

> And when he had opened the second seal, I heard the second beast say, Come and see.
>
> And there went out another horse that was red: and power was given to him that sat thereon to take peace from the earth, and that they should kill one another: and there was given unto him a great sword.

The word "red" makes some people shout "communism." I am no friend of communism, but let me emphasize one thing every Bible student should do. He should ask himself the question, "Does it say that?" I learned to ask that question when I was a student of Dr. Herman Hoyt, past president of Grace Theological Seminary.

Now read it again. What does it say? It says this rider will take peace from the earth. That is simple enough. If there is no peace, there must be war. So this horse simply signifies war. That fits with the idea of conquering in verse 2.

Notice also it is no small war. It says in verse 4 "a *great* sword" and "take peace from the *earth.*" It looks like war on a worldwide scale. What a sad day for the human race when this superman comes offering himself as the answer to all their dreams—the man who will bring peace at last—the man who will solve all the world's problems! But he starts with terrible warfare. With such warfare we are not surprised to find that famine follows next.

THE THIRD SEAL
AND THE BLACK HORSE OF FAMINE

Verses 5 and 6:

> And when he had opened the third seal, I heard the third beast say, Come and see. And I beheld, and lo a black horse; and he that sat on him had a pair of balances in his hand.

> And I heard a voice in the midst of the four beasts say, A measure of wheat for a penny, and three measures of barley for a penny; and see thou hurt not the oil and the wine.

The language used here suggests exorbitant food prices which could only result from severe food shortages. This indicates famine.

Jesus warned his followers (in Matt. 24:3 and 7) that one of the signs of His return would be famines in various places. So it appears that famines will already be stalking the earth at the time of the rapture of the saints. Right after that when the Antichrist is consolidating his world-dictatorship and war is rampant, famine will be widespread.

Do you realize that famines are already taking millions of lives in various countries and before long it will get much worse. One writer states that by the year 2000 this earth will have about seven billion people but well over half of them will starve to death. Imagine that! In a time of scientific and technological advancement heretofore unknown in history, more people are expected to starve than all the people alive at this moment. All of this must mean the second coming of Christ is very near.

We come now to the last of the four horsemen in verses 7 and 8.

THE FOURTH SEAL
AND THE PALE HORSE OF DEATH

> And when he had opened the fourth seal, I heard the voice of the fourth beast say, Come and see.
>
> And I looked, and behold a pale horse: and his name that sat on him was Death, and Hell followed with him. And power was given unto them over the fourth part of the earth, to kill with sword, and with hunger, and with death, and with the beasts of the earth.

ONE BILLION PEOPLE WILL DIE

One-fourth of the world's population will die from the sword (that's the war of v. 4) and with hunger (that's the famine of v. 6) and with wild beasts. This last item was not mentioned before. Perhaps the animals will become rabid. At any rate, they will become ferocious and attack people to the point of killing them.

Between war, famine, and wild beasts, approximately one-fourth of the world's population will die. The population of the world is now four billion. When a few hundred million Christians are evacuated to heaven, the world will still have approximately four billion—assuming the Lord returns before very long. So one-fourth would be approximately one billion. What an unspeakable catastrophe!

This will be the worst catastrophe to strike the human race in all of human history. Even the universal flood of Noah did not destroy nearly so many people. But this is just the beginning of the seven-year tribulation period which Jesus calls the worst in all history—past, present or future (Matt. 24:21). I'm glad that I'm sure

TRUE BELIEVERS WILL NOT BE HERE

Remember the Church (made up of all true believers) went to heaven in chapter 4. At this point they have already played in the harp orchestra and sung in the heavenly choir *before* the Lord broke the first seal. The Antichrist as the rider on the white horse makes his public bid for power only *after* the breaking of the first seal. The sequence of events here clearly indicates the Church will not be here during the special seven-year period of terrible tribulation. Anyone interested further in this subject should obtain a cassette copy of my sermon entitled: "Will the Church Go through the Tribulation?"

Look with me now at the story of

THE FIFTH SEAL
AND THE TRIBULATION MARTYRS

Verses 9-11:

And when he had opened the fifth seal, I saw under the altar the souls of them that were slain for the word of God, and for the testimony which they held:

And they cried with a loud voice, saying, How long, O Lord, holy and true, dost thou not judge and avenge our blood on them that dwell on the earth?

And white robes were given unto every one of them; and it was said unto them, that they should rest yet for a little season, until their fellowservants also and their brethren, that should be killed as they were, should be fulfilled.

Please observe that these people were killed. Verse 11 says "... that should be killed as they were. ..." Notice also that they were "slain for the word of God, and for the testimony which they held." In other words, they are martyrs for the Lord. They cry out to God to do something about what is happening on the earth and they are told to wait a little while. God will indeed intervene in due time. But temporarily the devil's christ is killing all those who will not give their political allegiance and their spiritual worship to him.

Please note carefully and do not be confused: this passage has nothing to do with the Church or Christians of past centuries who were martyred for their faith in Christ. All of them went to heaven in verse 1 of chapter 4 and are at this very moment watching and participating in the coronation ceremony in heaven.

The ones described in verses 9 through 11 are the martyrs of the tribulation period, killed by the Antichrist. They are saved and will enter heaven in chapter 7. We shall meet them again specifically in chapters 7, 13 and 20.

THE SIXTH SEAL
AND THE WRATH OF GOD

At this point the Lamb (that is, the Lord in heaven) breaks the sixth seal and there follows an awful and awesome outpouring of the wrath of God in righteous judgment upon a world that is worshiping the devil and his christ.

Verses 12-17:

> And I beheld when he had opened the sixth seal, and, lo, there was a great earthquake; and the sun became black as sackcloth of hair; and the moon became as blood;
> And the stars of heaven fell unto the earth, even as a fig tree casteth her untimely figs, when she is shaken of a mighty wind.
> And the heaven departed as a scroll when it is rolled together; and every mountain and island were moved out of their places.
> And the kings of the earth, and the great men, and the rich men,

and the chief captains, and the mighty men, and every bondman, and every free man, hid themselves in the dens and in the rocks of the mountains;

And said to the mountains and rocks, Fall on us, and hide us from the face of him that sitteth on the throne, and from the wrath of the Lamb:

For the great day of his wrath is come; and who shall be able to stand?

This will be a period when the wrath of God will be outpoured in a frightful unleashing of the forces of nature in a manner never before experienced by man. There will be an earthquake of such magnitude as to move mountains and islands off their bases. The people will see a black sun and a red moon. All the while there will be terrible thunderstorms, ferocious winds and frightening showers of meteors—perhaps from a comet whipping its tail across the path of planet Earth.

Right now, in all the freak weather conditions from tornadoes to floods, I do believe we are getting the very beginning of this final outpouring of God's judgment upon a wicked and rebellious world. It is part of God's preliminary warning to the human race of what is to follow for those who refuse to repent and be saved.

WHAT ABOUT THE LOVE OF GOD?

Did you notice in verse 17 that John, by divine inspiration, calls it "the great day of his wrath"? To be sure God is a God of love. He loved us so much He sent His Son to die in our place and stead, making it possible that anyone who receives Him by faith can be saved. That's infinite, marvelous, matchless love beyond compare. God is not willing that any should perish.

But the question is: What is the alternative for those who reject such love? The answer is: All those who reject God's love must face His wrath. It will do you no good to be angry or argumentative with me. I didn't write it. I'm just God's reporter. It is right there in His Word. As a preacher, I am obligated before God to warn men to "flee from the wrath to come" (Matt. 3:7). The choice is entirely yours—God's love or God's wrath.

144,000 JEWS SEALED

We want to get on with the coronation but John stops long enough to tell us about two special events in chapter 7. Read the first eight verses and you'll see that 144,000 Israelites (commonly called Jews) are sealed by an angel so they can't be hurt by the plagues. Every tribe is represented here and whether or not the number is symbolic, one thing is certain, God is making sure that some of Jesus' earthly kinsmen will be alive when He returns to reign on the throne of His father David. After all, the prophets foretold that Israel would be the head nation during the millennial reign of Christ. Whether or not they become flaming evangelists at this point is not clear. But they are sealed so they can't be destroyed in the coming judgments.

THE GREAT MULTITUDE OF ALL NATIONS

Beginning with verse 9, read to the end of the chapter. Here we have the story of the appearance of the tribulation martyrs in heaven. The 144,000 in the preceding verses were on earth. But this vast multitude of all nations is in heaven, having just now arrived—late, as it were, for the coronation ceremony. They missed the first numbers of the orchestra and the choir but they have arrived in time to see the King crowned.

There can be no question as to their identity if you read verse 14. The Greek language, which is the original language of this book, says, "These are they which came out of tribulation, the great one . . . ."

In every century, the followers of Christ have been persecuted and martyred somewhere in the world. With the satanic treatment of Christians in Russia and China during my lifetime, it can be said that there have been more martyrs in my generation than in any period of history, even though much of this bloody work has not been published. Even so, the worst blood bath is still to come during the tribulation—the great one!

In chapter 8, verse 1, we have an awesome and momentous scene.

> And when he had opened the seventh seal, there was silence in heaven about the space of half an hour.

THE SEVENTH SEAL

Finally the moment has come! The Lamb has broken the last seal. That means He will now open the title deed and declare possession of His property. That means God is going into action. He will intervene in the affairs of earth. Lucifer and his fake christ will be thrown out. So all heaven pauses breathlessly for a moment (a half-hour by earth's time) in great expectation. Then

SEVEN ANGELS WITH SEVEN TRUMPETS

step up to the "platform." Each in turn will blow his heavenly trumpet heralding the crowning of the King. If our heavenly bodies are capable of getting heavenly goose bumps, we will surely have them. The chills will run up and down our heavenly spines as we listen to the angels blow the trumpets. What a thrill!

Some years ago my friend, Dick Messner, now Director of Development for Grace College, and I were scheduled to appear before the high school student body in Leesburg, Indiana. I was to speak and Dick was to play his trumpet. I suggested that the program start by having Dick blow a blast on the trumpet that would immediately command the undivided attention of the students.

Dick is an expert and when he sounded the call, the audience was electrified. I happened to be watching a student whose attention was far from the stage. He was talking to a student behind him and was only partially seated in his seat. Well, when Dick blew his trumpet that student was so jarred he nearly fell off his seat. I wanted to laugh; it was so funny. When the angels blow their trumpets, it won't be funny, but it will be thrilling.

With the blowing of each trumpet in turn an awful judgment will befall the population of earth. But when the seventh trumpet is sounded and we are delirious with joy, the climactic announcement will be made as we see in verse 15, chapter 11:

> And the seventh angel sounded; and there were great voices in heaven, saying, The kingdoms of this world are become the king-

doms of our Lord, and of his Christ; and he shall reign for ever and ever.

Notice what we will do. We won't just sit there; we'll do something. We have just witnessed the crowning of the King of kings and it will be as natural as the singing of the birds for us to prostrate ourselves at His feet as we worship and adore Him.

Verses 16 and 17:

And the four and twenty elders, which sat before God on their seats, fell upon their faces, and worshipped God.

Saying, We give thee thanks, O Lord God Almighty, which art, and wast, and art to come; because thou hast taken to thee thy great power, and hast reigned.

We have a song we like to sing: "I want to be there when they crown Him King of kings." Well, this is how it will happen and if you love and trust Jesus as your personal Saviour and Lord, you'll be there. Otherwise, you won't be there. It's as simple as that.

Now briefly look at chapter 12 in your Bible. The woman clothed with the sun is Israel. The red dragon is Satan. The "man child, who was to rule all nations with a rod of iron" can be no one but Christ (see Rev. 19:15). He was caught up to heaven at the time of the ascension. The Israelites (the Jews) are preserved for 1,260 days in a mountain hideaway (probably Petra) some 100 miles south of Jerusalem. This three and one-half year period will be the second half of the tribulation period.

That brings us now to chapter 13 where John pauses long enough to tell us in great detail about

THE BEAST — THE ANTICHRIST — THE COMING WORLD RULER

Verses 1 and 2:

And I stood upon the sand of the sea, and saw a beast rise up out of the sea, having seven heads and ten horns, and upon his horns ten crowns, and upon his heads the name of blasphemy.

And the beast which I saw was like unto a leopard, and his feet were as the feet of a bear, and his mouth as the mouth of a lion: and the dragon gave him his power, and his seat, and great authority.

This world ruler arises out of the sea of humanity. He is a man. Daniel tells us he is the head of one of ten countries (Rev. 17:11).

In verse 2 we find the empires of world history and Bible prophecy all wrapped up in one world system and handed over to this false superman. He gets everything given to him by Satan. Satan who is the god of this world has them because he stole them, not because he owns anything. So it says, ". . . the dragon gave him his power, and his seat [throne], and great authority."

HIS DEATH AND RESURRECTION

Verses 3 through 6:

> And I saw one of his heads as it were wounded to death; and his deadly wound was healed: and all the world wondered after the beast.
> And they worshipped the dragon which gave power unto the beast: and they worshipped the beast, saying, Who is like unto the beast? who is able to make war with him?
> And there was given unto him a mouth speaking great things and blasphemies; and power was given unto him to continue forty and two months.
> And he opened his mouth in blasphemy against God, to blaspheme his name, and his tabernacle, and them that dwell in heaven.

When you read that one of his heads was wounded to death, you can understand it more readily if you are a Pennsylvania Dutchman like myself. It simply means: They killed him dead! But to the utter astonishment of the whole world he doesn't stay dead. That's what it means when it says "his deadly wound was healed."

This is an imitation of the death and resurrection of the true Christ. When Christ arose, the world didn't believe it. But when the false christ does it, they will believe it.

It should be mentioned that Satan has no power but what God allows him. At this point God will allow him the power to bring back the Antichrist from the dead.

The purpose is to force the people to declare themselves; that is, to make a choice and publicly reveal their loyalties.

There'll be no atheists in that day. Every lost person will be forced to choose his god. He can accept the Antichrist (the beast), or he can accept the true Christ. If he accepts the false christ, he will irrevocably seal his doom in the fires of a devil's hell. (See chap. 14, vv. 9 through 11.) If he rejects the Antichrist, it will only be because he accepts the true Christ. In that case he will be killed by the Antichrist to join the saved tribulation martyrs.

Paul tells us in the second chapter of I Thessalonians that God will give them over to believe a lie. The lie is that the Antichrist is God. Remember, God is a God of love, the God of Calvary where Christ died so men need not perish. But when God has done all that He can do and they have not accepted His offer of eternal life in Christ, He has no further alternative but to turn them over to Satan and his false christ—whom they will now publicly choose.

Today many people, including some preachers and professing Christian laymen, deny the supernatural. They don't believe in God or Satan as real persons. They don't believe in heaven or hell as real places. They don't believe in miracles or the supernatural. They don't believe in the necessity of receiving Christ as their Saviour to redeem them from sin. Consequently, they are unsaved.

But when Satan brings the beast back from the dead, they will believe the lie and will accept the beast as their god and they will begin worshiping him.

Use your imagination to think how it might be: The whole world is having a period of mourning. Their superman whom they had hoped would finally solve all the world's problems is dead. The world's most famous funeral lasts for days while the world deeply mourns. All their hopes for a man who could build a dream world of peace and prosperity are now sealed in a casket. Television brings the funeral to most of the world's population, right into their living rooms.

Then suddenly they are stunned! The corpse has shattered the casket and is now alive and going into action. He snaps his fingers and the lightning flashes. He speaks with great authority and the world falls at his feet. He demands that they worship him as God and they will. The world goes mad with joy as they say to each other, "How can you fight with a fellow like that?"

Lucifer is imitating God the Father; the beast is imitating Christ; and at this point the world as a whole is worshiping both these imposters. In verse 4, you understand, the dragon is Satan, alias Lucifer.

Now read verse 7 and the announcement of

ONE WORLD GOVERNMENT

And it was given unto him to make war with the saints, and to overcome them: and power was given him over all kindreds, and tongues, and nations.

The last sentence clearly indicates there will be one world government. The Antichrist will rule with supernatural satanic power as absolute dictator of earth.

All who reject him will be martyred. They are the saints of whom it is said that he "overcame" them. In other words, he killed them. As I pointed out in an earlier message, these are not the saints of the Church Age. They are already in heaven having been there since the first verse in chapter 4.

The dream of Wendell Wilkie who wrote a book back in the early 1940s called *One World* will come true. The dream of the United Nations will come true. The dream of many leaders of the World Council of Churches for one world government will come true—but not like they think. It will not be a democracy. It will be a dictatorship and the dictator will be the personification of the devil himself.

Now read verse 8 and observe carefully. This is the best verse in the Bible to prove that there will be

ONE WORLD CHURCH

There can be no question about it. One world church is in the making. It will be made up of all who worship Satan and his christ (the beast) and under penalty of death no other worship will be allowed.

When we see all the plans being laid in ecclesiastical world circles for a world church, and when we actually see churches worshiping Satan, we can only conclude that the coming of the Lord must be very near indeed.

Now let us look at verse 11 where we are introduced to the third person of the satanic trinity called

ANOTHER BEAST OR THE FALSE PROPHET

Verses 11 through 15:

And I beheld another beast coming up out of the earth; and he had two horns like a lamb, and he spake as a dragon.

And he exerciseth all the power of the first beast before him, and causeth the earth and them which dwell therein to worship the first beast, whose deadly wound has healed.

And he doeth great wonders, so that he maketh fire come down from heaven on the earth in the sight of men,

And deceiveth them that dwell on the earth by the means of those miracles which he had power to do in the sight of the beast; saying to them that dwell on the earth, that they should make an image to the beast, which had the wound by a sword, and did live.

And he had power to give life unto the image of the beast, that the image of the beast should both speak, and cause that as many as would not worship the image of the beast should be killed.

Here John calls him another beast. In Revelation 19:20, John calls him the false prophet. His job is to imitate the work of the Holy Spirit. He tries to get the people to worship the devil's christ just as the Holy Spirit tries to get the people to worship the true Christ, and the beast is possessed of supernatural satanic power just like the first beast.

The devil's trinity is a counterfeit of the Holy Trinity. Satan is counterfeiting God the Father; and Antichrist is counterfeiting God the Son, and the False Prophet is counterfeiting God the Holy Spirit. As God's Christ has a kingdom, so the Antichrist is given a kingdom—a counterfeit kingdom that will be allowed to operate under Antichrist for exactly 42 months (v. 5) or 1,260 days (chap. 11, v. 3) which is, of course, three and one-half years (Dan. 7:25). And as Christ has a church called his bride, so Lucifer has a church for his christ whom God pictures in chapter 17 as a scarlet harlot. Lucifer is imitating

God in every way possible. He is phony all the way, but he does deceive untold billions of mortals and therefore he is called the great deceiver.

Did you notice the last line of verse 14 tells us how the Antichrist was killed? They didn't shoot him. Nobody threw a hand grenade or planted a bomb. It says he had a wound by a sword. Somebody stabbed him but, of course, he didn't stay dead.

In verses 14 and 15 we are told about

THE IMAGE OF THE BEAST

With this world hero now in control as Satan's superman, the order is given to build an image of the Antichrist. According to Daniel 9:27 and Matthew 24:15 this will take place in the Jewish Temple in Jerusalem, right in the middle of the seven year tribulation period. Some time between now and then the temple must be rebuilt. There is no temple now. The last one was destroyed by the Roman army under General Titus in A.D. 70 when the city of Jerusalem was leveled.

When that image is unveiled in the temple, undoubtedly the world will have a special holiday to celebrate the event. And what a shocking surprise! As hundreds of millions watch on television, they will see the image come alive and begin to walk and talk. Now if anybody has been holding back in his full allegiance politically or full commitment spiritually, this will be the final factor to convince him. He will now unreservedly give himself totally to the devil, believing the great lie—that Satan is God.

Let me emphasize again, Satan does not have the power of life. Only God has that; after all, He made Lucifer in the first place. But for reasons that I explained earlier, God will at this point allow Satan whatever power is necessary to force all mortals to make a choice and stand by that choice. Even with all that has happened up to this point, maybe there will be some individuals who are unconvinced. They might say, "We are scientists. We only believe that which you can prove in a laboratory, that which can be checked with a microscope, a telescope, a slide rule or a computer." But when the image comes alive, their arguments collapse and they fall before him in worship. So that brings us now to

THE MARK OF THE BEAST

Verses 16 through 18:

And he causeth all, both small and great, rich and poor, free and bond, to receive a mark in their right hand, or in their foreheads:

And that no man might buy or sell, save he that had the mark, or the name of the beast, or the number of his name.

Here is wisdom. Let him that hath understanding count the number of the beast; for it is the number of a man; and his number is Six hundred threescore and six.

Everybody is talking about 666. If you play with numbers you can find it in the name of Kissinger, in the Pope's crown and on the walls of the Kremlin. It also appears today on many license plates on vehicles in Jerusalem. So what does that prove? Nothing!

There can only be one devil's christ. He will come out of the old Roman empire. He will be a man. He will be the head of a country. He will be energized by Satan. He will rule the world. He will set himself up as God and the world will worship him. Beyond these basic facts it is difficult to prove anything else as to his identity. Will he be Judas incarnate? Will he be Jewish? It is impossible to say with certainty.

Six is man's number. He was made on the sixth day. It is just short of the perfect number seven. Man can never be perfect and therefore can never save himself. But now he takes to himself man's god in three persons—the Devil's trinity—hence 666.

It appears to me that it will be impossible for believers to positively identify the Antichrist before we leave for heaven. The Bible teaches that we should look for the coming of God's Christ. The New Testament is full of warnings telling us to look, watch, be ready, and so forth. It's a trick of Satan to get our eyes off of Christ and onto the Antichrist. Let's not be tricked by the great deceiver. Let's keep our eyes on the sky for His coming draweth nigh.

But God does want us to know certain things and that's why all this was written. We are told in this passage that everyone will be required to receive the mark of the beast in his right hand or in his forehead. The choice of location suggests that we must take it literally—just like the ration stamps of the second world war. Those gas coupons were not figurative.

It appears simple enough. When the Antichrist comes to power, he will order polling places open all over the world; and every person on earth will then be ordered to come and "vote." All those who appear will do so because they have joined the new world party and have given full allegiance to the new ruler. They will be given some kind of indelible identification in one of two places (right hand or forehead) to show publicly their choice of allegiance.

All who refuse to take the mark will be doing so because they refuse to worship Satan. They will not be allowed to buy or sell anything and they will be killed if they can be found. Vast multitudes will be killed. Some will escape as we shall see in a later message when we talk about those who repopulate the millennial earth.

LET US PRAY

Our Heavenly Father, we thank Thee for Thy word. We shudder to think of what is coming on this earth after the true Christians leave, but, Lord, help us now to do all we can so that as many as possible may be saved. Help us to anticipate the day when Jesus shall come and we shall rise to meet Him in the air. Grant, O Lord, that if there is anyone here tonight unsaved, he will ask the Saviour to come into his heart before it is too late.

So, Lord, do a mighty work in hearts. Help us spread the Gospel around the world through the ministry of missionaries and through the faithfulness of those at home, in prayer, in giving, and in personal witnessing. May many come to know Jesus before this age closes. The world government is in the making; the world church is in the making; and certainly it cannot be long until You must come and take us home. So we pray that every person here shall be ready. May not one be missing when the trumpet sounds and we hear the shout of command from the lips of the Commander-in-Chief Himself, to rise and meet Him in the air. O, Lord, may it be tonight. We pray it in Jesus' name. Amen.

V

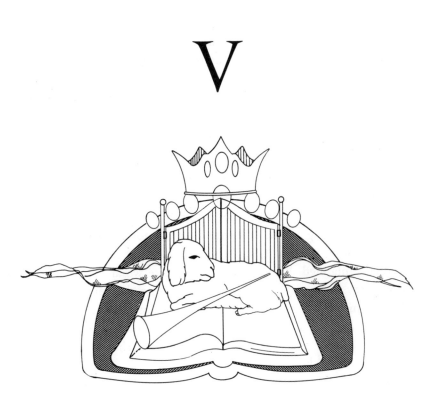

The Seven
Last Plagues

REVELATION 15 and 16

Tonight's subject is a very unpleasant one—the darkest scene this side of hell. It is pictured in the sixteenth chapter of the Book of Revelation. I want to expound that chapter, but first I want to call your attention to two verses from the lips of Jesus Himself. He was speaking of this period in the twenty-fourth chapter of Matthew, verses 21 and 22.

For then shall be great tribulation, such as was not since the beginning of the world to this time, no, nor ever shall be.

And except those days should be shortened, there should no flesh be saved: but for the elect's sake those days shall be shortened.

The meaning is not that the period. will be shorter than planned. It simply means the period will be short—having a definite stopping point. It certainly does not mean that when God sees how terrible it is, He is going to cut it shorter than He originally planned. We can say this because we are told exactly to the day how long it will be, so there is no shortening of it at the last minute. It simply means except those days are short in number—having a fixed, cutoff point, nobody could live through it. But for the sake of "the elect," that is, the Jews, those days shall be limited in number.

In this passage Jesus is referring to the period which we are now about to describe. John records the awful details in Revelation 15 and 16. In chapter 15 we have the introduction and heavenly setting. In chapter 16 we have the detailed account of the final outpouring of the wrath of a holy God on a world that is in rebellion, having given itself to the worship of Satan and his christ, called the Beast or Antichrist.

THE HEAVENLY SETTING

Look now at the first verse of chapter 15.

And I saw another sign in heaven, great and marvellous, seven angels having the seven last plagues; for in them is filled up the wrath of God.

Please notice in verse 2 that the martyrs of the tribulation are present in the heavenly scene. Compare the language of this verse with 13:15-18 and you'll know this is true. This is significant!

We believe the seven last plagues take place during the second half of the tribulation period and that they run through the entire three and one-half years. If that is correct, then the first plague would begin about the same time the image of the Antichrist is unveiled in the temple in Jerusalem and the last one would take place about the same time as the destruction of the city of seven hills (headquarters for the world church) and just before the battle of Armageddon. Undoubtedly this seventh plague has a large part to play in both of those catastrophies.

Read the rest of chapter 15 for yourself, but now let's focus our attention on chapter 16 and

THE SEVEN LAST PLAGUES

This is the third group of sevens since this period started in chapter 6. First we had seven seals, then seven trumpets, and now seven plagues. They are called the seven *last plagues* because this is the final climactic outpouring of God's wrath.

Seven angels each carry a bowl or a vial that is filled to overflowing with the wrath of an angry God. Why is He angry? Because the whole world, it seems, has given its spiritual worship to Lucifer, God's enemy, and to Lucifer's christ. They are acknowledging him as God. Therefore, God is going to pour out judgments upon this earth the like of which men have never experienced. He will now open the artillery of heaven and bombard and lambast this wicked world with unspeakable judgments.

It is an awful scene, and I would like to skip it; but I cannot. God wrote it; it is my job to warn people to flee from the wrath to come. Any person here tonight who does not know Christ as Saviour and who willfully rejects Christ stands a very excellent chance of being on the earth when this scene takes place.

By the same token, if you have accepted Christ as your Saviour, it will be impossible for you to be here. All those who love the Lord will go up at the Lord's appearing and that takes place in the first verse of chapter 4. The church in heaven sings the song of redemption in chapter 5. So here in chapter 16, we do not find the church on earth. That's good news. But knowing as we do what is coming, we have a great concern for those who are lost. We ought to be interceding with the Lord for our loved ones, for our friends and our neighbors, that God will work a mighty work in us and through us and around us, so that others who are still unsaved may come to Christ before it is too late.

Three and a half years after the Lord comes for His saints, this scene will take place. It takes place in the second half of the tribulation period, the period that is exactly two times 1,260 days. That is two times 42 months, or two times three and one-half years, or a total of seven years. Daniel calls it a week of years. There is no question about the length of it. All these figures are given in various Bible passages.

So, if you are ready now, let's look at the individual plagues as John records them, one at a time, in chapter 16.

Verse 1:

> And I heard a great voice out of the temple saying to the seven angels, Go your ways, and pour out the vials of the wrath of God upon the earth.

The seven angels mentioned here are, I believe, the same seven angelic beings we met in 1:4, 4:5, 5:6, and 8:2. They are waiting near the throne of heaven, ever on the alert, ready to go into action and carry out God's command. In this case that command is to dump a bowl of God's judgment on the earth.

THE FIRST PLAGUE — SORES (HEALTH)

Verse 2:

> And the first went, and poured out his vial upon the earth; and there fell a noisome and grievous sore upon the men which had the mark of the beast, and upon them which worshipped his image.

God is the author of good health. He made the body and all the laws that govern its well-being. The human body is the crowning display of the power of the Creator. Imagine a machine that heals its own cuts or dented fenders like our bodies do. No car out of Detroit does that. How often do we remember to thank Him?

In our passage here we are told God will, by supernatural power and decree, order the health of Satan-worshiping mortals to be "turned off." When this plague falls upon the earth, the bodies of individuals who have given their allegiance to the devil's christ are going to be covered with awful, annoying, obnoxious, grievous, painful sores. There will be no cure and there will be no relief. All the doctors and all the nurses and all the miracle drugs will be of no avail. God is the Creator of the body in the first place and He is also the author of health. Now He has decreed at this point that the mortals who are worshiping the Antichrist will, by divine power, be covered with incurable sores. And so it will be. The suffering of humanity engaged in worshiping the Antichrist has just begun. What a horrible experience will be Plague Number 1!

Notice that only those who received the mark of the beast are hurt by these plagues. Back in chapter 13 we were told that during this period, all mortals on earth would be required to register, indicating that they had joined the world party and had given their political allegiance and their spiritual worship to this man who has set himself up as God. All those who did so were given an identification mark either on the forehead, or in their right hand.

Now all those who have that mark have identified themselves with the Antichrist with a seal that can never be broken. They have made their choice, their doom is sealed forever. Those who accept that seal will have confirmed their choice, and it can never be changed. They will spend eternity in hell (see 14:9-11). Meanwhile these plagues will befall them while they are still on this earth.

Do you also remember in the seventh chapter a group of 144,000 Israelites were sealed so they couldn't be hurt by the plagues? So it is clear that these plagues of judgment are intended for those people who have given their political allegiance and spiritual worship to the devil and the Antichrist.

THE SECOND PLAGUE
FILTHY OCEANS (FRESH AIR)

Verse 3 gives us the second of these plagues.

And the second angel poured out his vial upon the sea; and it became as the blood of a dead man: and every living soul died in the sea.

What a catastrophe that will be! Men have failed to thank God for the sea. The oceans of the world are one of the great gifts that God gave to the human race. Did you ever stop to think about that? The oceans are a great perpetual purification plant for this old earth. During all the centuries since man has been on the earth, he has been dumping his slop and sewage so that the rain washes it down the rivers into the sea. But the sea is always fresh and clean. God ordained that the "seven seas" should be a perpetual purification plant to keep this old earth clean. Now God is going to "turn it off."

Men haven't appreciated what He has done. They have not thanked Him. At this point, they are not even recognizing His existence. They have declared that the God of the Bible is dead. They said they didn't believe in a supernatural being somewhere in space called God.

But now the true and living omnipotent God will assert Himself. It is as if He will say, "All right, let's see how long you can get along without me." Then one by one He turns off the great benefits He has provided for man. In the first plague, it's their health. Now it's the fresh air.

When the great purification plant called ocean or sea becomes a vile, filthy cesspool, "like the blood of a dead man," you can be sure the winds will pick up the stench and sweep it around the world.

Men who are covered with painful boils must now also inhale air that is too vile and foul to breathe; but there is no escape. The whole planet is polluted beyond anything we can imagine.

Even today man is threatening to destroy the ocean life by his indiscriminate dumping of poisons into the sea. But the judgment we read about in Revelation 16 is something that happens very quickly by supernatural decree.

What an awful day when the judgments of a holy God begin to fall on a world that has rejected the true Christ and has given itself to the worship of the devil's christ. Obviously both the devil and the Antichrist will be helpless to answer the prayers of their worshipers when God has ordered this whole sequence of judgments.

And that brings us to verse 4 and

THE THIRD PLAGUE
DRINKING BLOOD (FRESH WATER)

Verses 4 through 7:

> And the third angel poured out his vial upon the rivers and fountains of waters; and they became blood;
>
> And I heard the angel of the waters say, Thou art righteous, O Lord, which are, and wast, and shalt be, because thou hast judged thus.
>
> For they have shed the blood of saints and prophets, and thou hast given them blood to drink; for they are worthy.
>
> And I heard another out of the altar say, Even so, Lord God Almighty, true and righteous are thy judgments.

Jesus tells us that the drinking water of earth will be changed to blood. It doesn't say "as blood"; it says "they became blood." In the second plague the oceans turned to something "*like* the blood of a dead man." I have never seen the blood of a dead man. I have no desire to see the blood of a dead man. But I have a good enough imagination. John says that not a living thing could live in the sea—that is what it says. In the third plague we are told God is going to change the fresh water. He has dealt with the salt water, now He is going to change the drinking water of earth to blood. Can you imagine what it will be like when men's bodies are covered with incurable sores for which there is no relief, the air is filled with a stench that is so vile they can hardly breathe, and when they rush to the faucet to get a drink of water they will get a glass full of blood. Imagine how they will hurry out to a neighbor on the farm who has one of those old-fashioned pumps. They want to pump a drink of good, cold water out of the well, but when they swing the pump handle, they will discover that the pump is pumping blood. They will rush to the mountains where there is a pure, sparkling spring-water fountain bursting forth from the rocks. They can't wait to get some good cold water, but to their utter horror, they will discover that the spring has turned to blood.

In desperation now, they will turn to the river, the last source they can think of for water. They are ready to drink anything just so they can get some water. And to the river they go. But when they get there, they will discover the river, too, has turned to blood. What a horrible day to be alive.

This sounds like a horror movie. But I didn't write it. It's God's Word. I am not the author; I am just God's reporter. God says it; I am reading it to you. I hope you have your Bible so you can see for yourself what it says. "The third angel poured out his vial upon the rivers and fountains of waters: and they became blood."

Now look again at verse 5. The angel says, "Thou art righteous, O Lord, which art, and wast, and shalt be, because thou hast judged thus." The three verb phrases used here indicate the eternity of God.

The angel is saying that the eternal God is righteous and holy in such terrible judgments because of the awful sins of mortals. Verse 6 tells us they are getting what they deserve.

Remember the martyrs back in chapter 6 who arrived at the heavenly throne and cried out: "O Lord, how long will you wait to intervene and bring judgment upon the earth; for the devil and his christ are running the world and men are worshiping Satan." That is the essence, at least. The martyrs were crying out for revenge against those who were murdering people who rejected the devil and his christ. And now, at last, the revenge is coming. The Lord says vengeance belongs to Him, and at this point He pours out the most horrible plague this side of hell as drinking water is turned to blood.

Most people do not realize what a tremendous blessing God gave the human race when He gave us drinking water. How often do we remember to thank Him?

I want to tell you a story from my own experience to help you realize what a gigantic operation God has going continually to keep us supplied with fresh water.

Some years ago, I was involved in a number of business enterprises in eastern Pennsylvania about the time I was elected to the ministry. Among other things, I was raising a lot of chickens. The late Coble Grimes of "College Hill Poultry"—a man who made a million dollars in the broiler business—talked me into the business. By the way, he originated the idea of selling cut-up poultry direct to the housewife and he became wealthy in the process. During the great depression of the '30s many businesses failed, but Mr. Grimes' business grew so fast, he became a millionaire.

One summer I worked in his dressing plant trying to earn a few dollars to go to college. Jobs were mighty scarce and I was glad to have one even though I had to take the feathers off of one chicken every minute to keep the job. And that was by hand too—picking machines had not yet been invented.

That's how I got acquainted with Mr. Grimes. Now it's years later and the broiler business had grown so fast he couldn't get enough chickens to supply his markets. So he talked me into quitting school-teaching and going into the broiler business.

With the help of my father-in-law, I built the first large, new, commercial broiler house in the state of Pennsylvania. Before the Lord got me out of that business, I had raised about a half million chickens.

Meanwhile, E. E. Meyer, a relative and a reputable insurance man who wanted to retire, talked me into being his successor. So I operated the Meyer Real Estate and Insurance Agency.

In the midst of all this, I was elected into the ministry. It was called the free ministry because preachers were not paid; they were expected to earn their own living.

We lived in Lebanon, Pennsylvania, where I took care of the real estate and insurance office. Occasionally, I drove out to the chicken farm to see how many chickens had died that day and at night I studied the Bible. It wasn't long, however, until the strain began to take its toll. I was on the verge of stomach ulcers. The doctor said, "Move out into the country and get yourself a riding horse." So I did.

I didn't have any money. But I had a friendly banker and a few friends. And by working extremely long days, I was able to do what I set my mind to. I found a large, run-down farm that I thought would suit my purpose. After a few weeks of negotiating with the owner, I bought it. It looked terrible. It was really run-down, as the Pennsylvanians would describe it. My wife and I sanded floors, painted the house, planted a new lawn, and surrounded it all with a white board fence.

But the long lane needed to be rebuilt, some dead trees needed to be bulldozed out, ditches needed filling and I had my heart set on a farm pond—which in those days was a rare thing. When I asked a contractor what all that would cost, he took my breath away by the price he quoted. My answer to him was, "For that price, I could buy a bulldozer and do it myself." So I did.

I went to the bulldozer people to shop for a bulldozer. I told the man I wanted to buy a bulldozer and keep it three months. After that I wanted him to sell it for me. The loss in price would be the cost of my work. All the figures were agreed upon. I paid $500 down and agreed to pay another sum in a few weeks when some of my chickens went to market.

When I got home that night feeling I had had a great day, I told my wife, "I bought a bulldozer."

She said, "You did what?"

"I bought a bulldozer."

"What did you use for money?" So I explained the arrangement.

A few days passed and one evening when I came home, I was suddenly as excited as a boy with a new toy. There it was—standing in the barnyard—a beautiful, shiny, new bulldozer.

I had never driven a bulldozer in my life. But they do come with instruction books. So I read them. Then I climbed into the seat and pressed the right buttons and what do you know! That monster could purr like a kitten or growl like a mountain lion. It obeyed my every command.

And oh, what power! I could pull the throttle and make that mighty diesel engine vibrate with power. In two minutes I could raise an iron "hand" and push down a high tree that took God 20 years to put there. What a great feeling to have such power in one's hands! I think every would-be dictator ought to run a bulldozer. And by the way, I have never had stomach ulcers since.

Well, I couldn't wait to get started. So I drove that machine around the barn and down into the meadow to build a dam.

Weeks later it was finished. It consisted of a hole in the ground, one acre in size and ten feet deep. The breast was seventy feet thick at the bottom. It had a three-to-one slope inside and a two-to-one slope on the back side. It had a stand-pipe and a spillway. It even had a small island. The only thing it didn't have was water. There was not a drop in sight. There was neither a stream nor a spring.

I remember, as I was putting the last finishing touches on the masterpiece of my creation, feeling something like an artist must feel. Then I looked up and saw my neighbor standing on the bank roaring with laughter.

When I asked him why he was laughing, he said, "What do you think you are doing?"

My simple answer, "I'm building a dam."

His next question: "What do you expect to use for water?"

I decided to keep him wondering as I replied, "The Lord will provide."

Now lest you think I was as crazy as he thought, let me hasten to tell you: I wasn't quite as foolish as it would have appeared. You see, I had expert advice. It was all engineered on the basis of information received from Pennsylvania State College. I had faith in their expertise and that's what I was depending on.

They had told me that enough rainfall drops from the sky in Lebanon County on every ten acres of ground to maintain a pond with a minimum of six foot depth—apart from streams or springs. Of course, it had to be lined with clay to be waterproof.

Well, I had plenty of clay and I had about seventy acres of drainage basin. So I trusted those who had the answers, and I believed I had built a dam. I am delighted to tell you that about six weeks later, my pond had two million gallons of H_2O and there was so much water that the overflow pipe couldn't handle it all. The rest was rushing over the wide spillway just as planned.

But where did all that water come from? The answer is: God provided it. And His provisions stagger the imagination. You see, God is operating—all the time, day and night, seven days a week, around the clock and around the year, summer and winter—a tremendous evaporation plant. Every second He is lifting multiplied millions of tons of water from the surface of the oceans high into the sky.

He doesn't have any big pumps, no big power plants; He just lifts it silently by His mighty power out of the seven seas and hangs it in the sky. Imagine that! If you didn't know this to be true, you would surely think it's a fairytale. Remember the sea is salt but He doesn't take the salt along; He leaves the salt behind. He needs that in the ocean to operate His purification plant. And, of course, we don't want the salt in our drinking water anyway.

So He leaves the salt behind, but He takes the fresh water. He parks it up there in the sky and then He starts the winds blowing. They blow God's magic water tanks called clouds over the land. At that point the process that was evaporation is now reversed. We call it condensation. It falls on the mountains. It falls on the farms. It falls in the valleys. It falls in the cities. Much of it soaks into the earth. People pump it out. The springs flow from the mountains; the rivers flow from the hills and the cities, and the farms all get their fresh water—from God.

By the way, I didn't sell that bulldozer as planned. My neighbor wanted me to build a pond for him. And that was the beginning of yet another business—excavating business. In the next two years I built more than sixty similar ponds throughout eastern Pennsylvania. And God filled every one of them.

He brought enough water from the Atlantic Ocean not only to fill my ponds, but to water every plant and every tree all over the entire state of Pennsylvania, New Jersey, New York, Ohio, and so on. What a gigantic water business God is operating! Don't forget to thank Him.

If you don't appreciate water, take a long ride into the desert without it or trying taking a bath with sand. God surely knew what He was doing when He invented water.

And, by the way, water proves there is a God. The head of a chemical laboratory told me that. He said, "Every liquid when frozen contracts and becomes heavier except water. If that were not true, life could not exist on the earth."

I told him I needed an explanation. So he continued, "If ice were heavier than water, the surface of the oceans in freezing climates would turn to ice and then settle to the bottom. This process would continue in rapid succession until the ocean became one big block of ice and the earth then would become a desert." So God passed a law but made one exception in the case of water for man's sake.

He also told me that God ordered ice frozen out of salt water to leave the salt behind. So icebergs, even though they may be formed out of salt water are all fresh water. Amazing! Isn't God wonderful!

Returning to our account of the seven last plagues: Men have not thanked God for all His blessings including that of fresh water, so He will turn it all to blood.

Remember, as a whole, the human race has given its political allegiance and its spiritual worship to Satan and the Antichrist, having completely rebelled against the true God. So now God will pour out His righteous wrath in holy judgment as the inhabitants of earth are forced to drink blood.

One by one God turns off the blessings and turns on the plagues. We are ready now for

THE FOURTH PLAGUE
SEVERE BURNS (THE SUN)

Verses 8 and 9:

> And the fourth angel poured out his vial upon the sun; and power was given unto him to scorch men with fire.
>
> And men were scorched with great heat, and blasphemed the name of God, which hath power over these plagues: and they repented not to give him glory.

At this point, we are told that God is going to turn up the heat by turning up the power of the sun in such a way that it will affect these mortals who are worshiping the Antichrist. Their bodies will be covered with burns as if they had an awful sunburn or as if they were burned in a fire. This is horrible beyond words! If you have ever suffered from sunburn or other burns you have had a small sample of what John is here describing.

Remember, these individuals are now covered with sores. They can find no relief. The air is vile and foul from the wind blowing over the foul oceans. Drinking water has turned to blood. And now on top of that, the sun scorches them as if they were burned in a fire. What in the world are they going to do? What a horrible, horrible existence! What excruciating pain they will suffer at this point!

WHAT FUELS THE SUN?

But somebody says, "Wait a minute. You are not being scientific to think that God is going to turn up the sun. After all, the sun is out there in space taking care of itself." Is it? Just where does the sun get its fuel? Think about that for a while. All of you who have furnaces know that when a furnace runs out of fuel, the fire goes out. Anybody knows that! So exactly what is the source of fuel for the sun? Does the power and light company have high tension lines going out through space? Ninety-three million miles away is a ball of fire that is one million times bigger than this earth. For thousands of years the sun has been burning—ten thousand degrees hot at the surface, many times hotter in the interior and that great ball of fire has had no outside sources dumping fuel into it. Yet it goes on burning and burning and burning, century after century and millennium after millennium and the fuel is not exhausted.

On occasion, the old sun begins to spit flame far into space so that the fire shoots out into space a hundred thousand miles. And when that happens, the little people on the planet Earth say, "sun spots." Their radios don't work and they look at the brilliant display of light in the north and they call it the aurora borealis.

God is the source and author of all light and all power. And He is the one who made the sun; He is the one who decreed it should go on burning; it was He who decided that the sun should be our physical source of light and life on this earth. God is the author of it all. And in that day, He who made the sun is going to give the order and suddenly penetrating, harmful rays of the sun will produce burns on the bodies of those who have been worshiping the Antichrist.

Because it is ordered supernaturally, no protective shade, no roof—nothing will prevent the burns. At the present time it takes four feet of lead to stop the cosmic rays. In that day nothing will stop them.

The angel who is in charge of managing the sun will get the order to turn up the heat and in one way or another, it will surely happen.

In 1974 a book by two young scientists, Gribbin and Plagemann, called *The Jupiter Effect,* gave an alarming scientific warning of trouble in the sun that led many to think the time of the fourth plague might be only a few years away.

They said an unusual astronomical phenomenon would take place in 1982. All nine of the sun's major planets were to line up in one row, thus combining their gravitational pull on the sun in such a way as to pull flaming gases away from the sun and send streams of charged particles out into space past the planets themselves.

They said there would be huge storms on the sun resulting in cataclysmic changes on earth. Some of the possibilities they mentioned: an epidemic of earthquakes of major proportions, a change in the ionosphere, disruption of radio and television, weird lightings in the sky, a change in earth's prevailing winds, a change in rainfall and temperature patterns.

Fortunately for the human race, their predictions were only partially fulfilled. There have been terrible earthquakes and volcanic eruptions (like the big ones in Mexico and Mt. St. Helens in Washington). There have also been devastating changes in the weather patterns of the whole globe. God is warning the world, giving mankind a sample of what lies ahead.

These scientists did not speak from the viewpoint of a Bible teacher, but the things they described presented an amazing preview to what the Bible calls "tribulation—the great one!"

It could be that the rapture of the church is just ahead, inasmuch as the bride (the church) will be in heaven before the Biblical seven-year tribulation period starts. Take this as a warning: Trust Christ as your Saviour, and thus make sure of your reservation for heaven whenever or however your summons comes.

MEN WILL NOT REPENT

Take a look again at verse 9. Notice that even in the face of unspeakable judgments, evil men will not repent even though they realize by this time that Satan is helpless and that the true God of heaven has ordered the plagues. All they can do is curse and blaspheme God.

There is a point of no return in rejecting God's love and these people have reached it. They didn't thank God for the warm, life-giving rays of the sun and now God changes this blessing into a curse.

Take a look now at verse 10 as we consider

THE FIFTH PLAGUE
OVERWHEMING DARKNESS (LIGHT)

Verse 10:

And the fifth angel poured out his vial upon the seat of the beast; and his kingdom was full of darkness; and they gnawed their tongues for pain.

When the fifth angel pours out the contents of his vial, it falls on the kingdom of the Antichrist, resulting in great darkness.

Remember, they are covered with sores; the air is filled with stench; they must drink blood; they are covered with burns and now God turns out the light.

What a horrible day that will be! They didn't thank God for the light He created, but rather they rebelled against Him, cursed and blasphemed His name. Now He will temporarily turn it out.

I think we must take it literally because spiritually it could have no meaning. With the world worshiping Satan, the kingdom of the Antichrist has already been as dark spiritually as it could be. So when God brings darkness I think it involves physical darkness, just like all the other plagues are physical.

God is the author of light, so when He orders darkness, it will be so. God is the creator and sustainer of the sun; He also passed the law that causes a burning log or a red-hot wire (in a light bulb) to give off light.

Now He will supersede His natural law, and no electrician and no fireman will be able to produce light. Burning matches, flashlights, kerosene lamps, street lights, headlights—they will all be dark—very dark.

I think because of the supernatural order given by God, there will be total darkness as in a cave. I once visited the famous Carlsbad Caverns in New Mexico. It was the fulfillment of a boyhood dream. We went down 60 feet into the wonder world of stalactites and stalagmites. Of course, it was lighted all the way.

Then the guide announced that he was going to turn out the lights for one minute. "Don't panic," he said. "I'll turn the lights on again in 60 seconds. Now be perfectly quiet. Don't make a sound. When the lights are out, try to see your hand in front of you."

Suddenly there was darkness—utter darkness. I couldn't see my fingers even though I touched my eyeballs. Before the lights went on I had a "panicky" feeling—"What if those lights don't work?" I asked myself. Everybody was relieved when the place again was flooded with illumination.

Can you imagine how awful the experience would be to be suffering from all these plagues at one time and suddenly find oneself in total darkness unable to move about or to find anything?

So how will men respond? The next verse repeats what we already saw in verse 9.

Verse 11:

> And blasphemed the God of heaven because of their pains and their sores, and repented not of their deeds.

Notice that the plagues up to this point seem to be cumulative. They still have their sores; that was the very first plague. And in all this horrible agony, they bite their tongues as they blaspheme God. But they do not repent.

Some people think I shouldn't preach a terrible sermon like this. Once again, I must remind you, I didn't write it. God says it is going to happen! And it is the preacher's job to warn you to flee from the wrath to come. But if you do not accept Jesus Christ, if you do not receive the love that He offers, then you invite His wrath and you stand a very good chance of being alive three and one-half years after the church goes up—in which case you would surely experience these awful plagues. God does not want anyone to perish, but if you say "No, God, I do not want the offer You have made, I do not want Your Christ, I do not want Your salvation," then you have made the choice to reject His love and accept His wrath and you must bear the consequences. Just remember, you can't blame God. It was your own decision.

Look with me now at

THE SIXTH PLAGUE
PREPARATION FOR ARMAGEDDON

Verse 12:

> And the sixth angel poured out his vial upon the great river Euphrates; and the water thereof was dried up, that the way of the kings of the east might be prepared.

By this time the rivers have returned to water, not blood, as this verse tells us concerning the Euphrates. God will give the order and the dry river bed becomes a highway for the armies of the "kings of the east" (rising sun), that is, the East or the Orient.

According to verses 13, 14 and 16, Satan will send his demons to all the countries of the world with orders to bring their armies to the Valley of Armageddon where the last battle to be fought on the earth will take place. And we are told when it will happen—in "that great day of God Almighty."

In other words, when Christ as God appears in the sky, coming to reign as King of kings, Satan wants all the armies of earth marshaled against God. In chapter 19 we will see how it comes out.

Verses 13, 14, and 16:

> And I saw three unclean spirits like frogs come out of the mouth of the dragon, and out of the mouth of the beast, and out of the mouth of the false prophet.
>
> For they are the spirits of devils, working miracles, which go forth unto the kings of the earth and of the whole world, to gather them to the battle of that great day of God Almighty . . . . And he gathered them together into a place called in the Hebrew tongue Armageddon.

Now look at verse 15 where God has John put a warning and an invitation right in the middle of this horrible account. It's for those who read this awful story and decide they don't want to be here when it happens. They can prepare for sudden evacuation and thus escape the judgments to come. See Revelation 3:10 and John 5:24.

That brings us now to the seventh and last plague.

THE SEVENTH PLAGUE – MULTIPLE PLAGUE

Verse 17:

> And the seventh angel poured out his vial into the air, and there came a great voice out of the temple of heaven, from the throne, saying, It is done.

As the seventh angel pours out his vial, God announces, "That's all. No more!" But we look down to the planet Earth to see what happens, and we see a series of judgments like one mighty crescendo in a great finale terminating these awful plagues.

VOICES, LIGHTNINGS, THUNDERS, EARTHQUAKES

Verses 18 through 20:

> And there were voices, and thunders, and lightnings; and there was a great earthquake, such as was not since men were upon the earth, so mighty an earthquake, and so great.
>
> And the great city was divided into three parts, and the cities of the nations fell: and great Babylon came in remembrance before God, to give unto her the cup of the wine of the fierceness of his wrath.
>
> And every island fled away, and the mountains were not found.

All at once the air is filled with supernatural voices. It just might be that for once God lets mortals hear the voices of demons in the spirit world. I really don't know. But I'm sure it will be spooky and frightening.

The worst electrical storm of all time will now take place. I think every transformer on earth will be knocked out as well as every electrical motor and electronic device. I can imagine bolts of lightning jumping across the kitchen from the telephone to the television set. And, of course, with such lightning there will be unprecedented thunder. Bolt after bolt of lightning will be followed by one furious crack of thunder after another until buildings will shake.

The pent-up wrath of a holy God will be unleashed in such a supernatural, catastrophic display of His power that the very ground under their feet will begin to tremble until the inhabitants realize that the whole earth is shaking.

How do I know all this? We just read it. Verse 18 called it a great and mighty earthquake "such as was not since men were upon the earth." In other words, the most devastating earthquake of all time—past, present or future, will take place as part of plague number seven at the end of the seven-year tribulation period.

Verse 19 tells us that the cities of earth with their skyscrapers and high-rise apartments will topple and crumble into rubble.

What a mess! What suffering! What judgment! And the head-quarters of the Antichrist, called "great Babylon," will be destroyed at this time also. We'll learn more of this in the next message.

John speaks here of the "fierceness of his wrath," so you can be sure I didn't exaggerate in the above description.

Verse 20 tells us the earthquake will be so devastating that every island will be jolted off its foundation and slide into the sea and the mountains of earth will fall into the valleys. But that's not all.

THE GREAT FINALE
HAILSTONES LIKE BASKETBALLS

To top it all, while all this is happening, hailstones as big as basketballs will fall out of the sky. Verse 21 says they will be the weight of a talent. Authorities differ as to the exact weight of a talent. They vary from 50 to 100 pounds. Hailstones like that would utterly smash practically everything they would hit.

Thus God unleashes the fury of His power as He lambastes and bombards this wicked world with the artillery of heaven—pouring out the fierceness of His wrath in righteous judgment upon a world that has violated every law, spurned His love, rejected His Son, blasphemed His name, defied His Word, cursed His judgments and deified and worshiped His enemy, the devil himself. Jesus said it would be the most awful period of all history. And you can see why.

I am so glad that I am completely persuaded from my study of the Bible that I will not be here. The Body of Christ, His Bride, is made up of all true believers and they are one in Him. He will come in the air and snatch her away just before the tribulation period begins. I am so glad the Bible gives many guarantees that the church is not going into any part of the tribulation—not even the first half of the period—none of it. We have tribulation in the world, to be sure, but this is a special period for the express purpose of God pouring out His wrath on a world that has rejected Him. The Church, the Bride, did not reject Him, and at this point she is already in heaven. God will not be pouring out His wrath on His church. That is impossible. "For God hath not appointed us unto wrath . . ." (I Thess. 5:9). Revelation 3:10 says the same thing. Anyone wanting to know more of my reasons for making such a strong statement should hear my sermon called "Will the Church Go through the Tribulation?"

Well, that is God's account of the seven last plagues. If you don't like it, try arguing with God. But it would be foolish indeed for the creature to argue with the Creator. It would be far better to join the family of God. Accept His gracious provision for the salvation of your soul and be assured that He will be your Ark of Safety—a shelter in the time of storm.

It is not God's intention that His children should worry about "things coming to pass on the earth." He asks us to trust Him and relax in the assurance that before the tribulation period begins we will be singing in the heavenly choir and attending the coronation of the King. So don't neglect to make your reservation by asking Jesus to save you right now.

LET US PRAY

Our Heavenly Father, we praise Thee tonight for Thy Word, but we shudder to think what an awful day it will be when the judgments and wrath of a holy God are poured out upon a world that has rejected the true Christ and is worshiping the false christ. So tonight we would pray if there be any unsaved in the audience, the Holy Spirit of God may woo in that still, small voice, and bring the lost ones to Christ before it is too late.

Help any unsaved individual, O God, to pray the sinner's prayer and say, "Yes, Lord, be merciful to me a sinner. I know I am a sinner and I cannot save myself. Lord, You save me. Come into my heart and forgive my sin." The Bible says that "whosoever shall call upon the name of the Lord shall be saved" (Rom. 10:13). God, help any tonight who are unsaved to call upon Thee and settle the destiny of their souls.

Then, we pray for those of us who are saved. Lord, put Thy loving arm around each of Thy dear children tonight and love us close to Thy holy heart. Help us to see that we've got a job to do, and then energize us and empower us with the Holy Spirit to do that job, so that when Jesus comes and we pass through those pearly gates and walk down those streets of gold, we shall hear Him say, "Well done, thou good and faithful servant." May it be the experience of every Christian here tonight. We pray it in Jesus' name. Amen!

VI

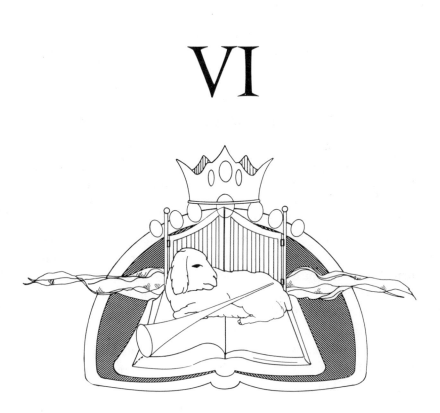

The Coming
World Church

✦

REVELATION 17 and 18

It is an awesome thing to stand before the people and speak for God. Yet, that is my task now. Indeed, every time a preacher stands in the pulpit, that is what he must do. God forbid that we should fail to declare the whole counsel of God.

MAD, SAD OR GLAD

As we move into chapter 17 of the Book of Revelation, we must deal with a very difficult and delicate subject—a subject that is extremely unpopular, and yet one that is of major importance because of the alternatives and consequences that are involved. The eternal destiny of the souls of millions is at stake.

If we sought only to please men, we would skip this message. However, since we must answer to God ultimately, we are compelled to proclaim the truth without fear or favor, knowing full well that some will hate us for it. When the truth is thus declared, inevitably, there are three reactions. Some people get mad, some get sad, and some get glad.

When Jesus exposed the hypocritical religious leaders of His day and told them who He really was, they were so angry that they tried to kill Him (John 10:31).

As far as I know, nobody has been that angry with me. Although one lady stalked angrily out of the church, pounding her fist in her hand, saying, "That Nathan Meyer makes me so *mad*!" However, not long after that she got saved. Now she's a dear friend. So if you leave this auditorium angry, I'll pray that God will use this experience to bring you to the knowledge of the Truth. And then I'll have one more friend.

When the rich young ruler came to Christ asking what he lacked in order that he might go to heaven, Jesus lost no time in telling him. His problem was money. That was the one thing that stood between him and heaven. So Jesus told him to go and get rid of it. Did he do it? No, he did not! It says he went away sorrowfully (Luke 18:23). He wasn't mad, just *sad*! For the sake of filthy lucre he rejected the unsearchable riches of Christ. He knew he had heard the truth, but he wasn't willing to do anything about it. It left him very sad.

Then there was the Ethiopian eunuch in Acts 8. Philip preached to him "The Truth"—Jesus. He accepted, requested baptism, and went on his way rejoicing. He was *glad*—very glad.

So it was and so it is. Somebody here will undoubtedly be glad, somebody will be sad, and somebody will be mad. In order that God may have maximum control of our minds and hearts in these sensitive moments, let's have a brief word of

PRAYER

O Lord, take complete control of our faculties and regulate our minds so that we will open them to the truth regardless of where it may lead. And then give spiritual gumption and backbone to those who hear that everyone may be willing to act wisely on the basis of the evidence which he observes.

Grant that none may be offended. Yet, at the same time give wisdom, strength, and courage to say what needs to be said, regardless of the consequences. Help me to say it all with a loving heart. Help everyone to listen with the intent of knowing the truth, cognizant of the fact that the truth alone can set men free.

May it all be for our good and for Thy glory! In Jesus' name we pray. Amen.

THE COMING WORLD CHURCH

We are now ready to expound chapters 17 and 18 of the Book of Revelation, continuing in our study of the future history of the world. This section deals with the final outcome of the world church—the devil's church—here described as a scarlet harlot.

We begin with chapter 17, verse 1.

> And there came one of the seven angels which had the seven vials, and talked with me, saying unto me, Come hither; I will shew unto thee the judgment of the great whore that sitteth upon many waters.

WHAT IS MEANT BY "WATERS"?

Notice this is the judgment—the final outcome—not the beginning, nor the middle, but the end. Observe the word "waters" at the end of this verse. Now let the Holy Spirit give us the explanation of "waters" in verse 15.

> And he saith unto me, The waters which thou sawest, where the whore sitteth, are peoples, and multitudes, and nations, and tongues.

WHO IS THE "WOMAN"?

This wicked, sensuous, sinful "woman" is brooding over the people, nations and languages of earth. Obviously, the woman is figurative and is not a literal female.

Now read on—verses 2 and 3.

> With whom the kings of the earth have committed fornication, and the inhabitants of the earth have been made drunk with the wine of her fornication.
>
> So he carried me away in the spirit into the wilderness: and I saw a woman sit upon a scarlet coloured beast, full of names of blasphemy, having seven heads and ten horns.

The "woman" of verse 3 must be connected with the Holy Spirit's explanation in verse 18.

> And the woman which thou sawest is that great city, which reigneth over the kings of the earth.

First we were told the woman broods over the multitudes of earth; now we find she is associated with a "great city." And notice this city is special in that it "reigneth over the kings of the earth." Kings are supposed to be at the top of the political power structure. But here is a city that reigns over kings. Imagine that! Who could this "woman" be who is quartered in a special city, reigning over the kings of the earth and brooding over the peoples of the whole world? We shall see.

THE SEVEN HEADS

We have additional information coming up. Notice the "seven heads" of verse 3. Compare this with verse 9 where we learn that "The seven heads are seven mountains [or hills], on which the woman sitteth."

THE CITY OF SEVEN HILLS

Now to put it all together. The woman is figurative. She is a system of some sort that is headquartered in a great city reigning over kings and that city is a city of seven hills. What city could that be? It is true that various cities like Istanbul have seven hills, but what schoolchild does not know that *the* "city of seven hills" is Rome.

I hasten to point out that in verse 3 the "woman" is said to be riding on the back of the beast. "The beast" in Revelation is always the Antichrist. "Another beast" in chapter 13, verse 11, is his helper who is called the false prophet in chapter 19, verse 20. In that passage, as we shall see later, both of these beasts are thrown into hell together. But *the beast* is always the false world ruler—the Antichrist—the devil's christ.

So the woman is riding on his back. Therefore, it would seem that he must have his headquarters in the city of seven hills, too. He is a man, energized by Satan and literally ruling the whole earth; she is a figurative woman—a system.

We have additional light shed on the subject in verses 4, 5 and 6.

> And the woman was arrayed in purple and scarlet colour, and decked with gold and precious stones and pearls, having a golden cup in her hand full of abominations and filthiness of her fornications:
> And upon her forehead was a name written, MYSTERY, BAB-YLON THE GREAT, THE MOTHER OF HARLOTS AND ABOMI-NATIONS OF THE EARTH.
> And I saw the woman drunken with the blood of the martyrs of Jesus: and when I saw her, I wondered with great admiration.

MYSTERY BABYLON

God calls her "Mystery, Babylon." In Romans 16:25 and Ephesians 3:3, Paul refers to the mystery of the true church where all believers are one in Christ. So here when all the related passages are considered in the light of the context, it appears that this is the mystery of the false church—the devil's church. Since the Antichrist has set himself up as God, demanding that he be worshiped as God (II Thess. 2:4 and Rev. 13:4, 8), it is quite clear that the church and state are one and that they have the same world headquarters.

The devil is a great counterfeiter. He himself is imitating God the Father; his False Christ is imitating God the Son; his False

Prophet is imitating God the Holy Spirit. These three make up the satanic trinity in imitation of the Holy Trinity. Then, too, as Christ has a church to worship Him, so Satan will have a church to worship him. In the fifth chapter of Ephesians, the Lord's church is pictured as a chaste, holy virgin. But the Bible pictures Satan's church as a scarlet harlot. So the "woman" pictured here is the false world church of the Great Tribulation period.

After the Jews finish building their temple (and this they surely will do some time between now and the middle of the seven-year tribulation period), it appears to me that the Antichrist will erect a palace in Jerusalem and set up his image in the Jewish temple (Dan. 11:45 and II Thess. 2:3-4). That's what Jesus was talking about in Matthew 24:15 (cf. Dan. 9:27).

But I believe that he starts out in Rome, the city of seven hills, and that his permanent capital (and the headquarters for his church) will be Rome. God calls it Babylon after the city in history where devil-worship first began. Historical Babylon was destroyed, never to be rebuilt according to the prophet Jeremiah (50:39 and 51:62). Current news media reports about rebuilding Babylon refer only to erecting a diminished semblance of the ancient walls and gates so the tourists will come and take pictures. This is also to include an attraction called "the Tower of Babel," we are told. It remains to be seen how much of this God will allow.

The religion of the Antichrist is the same work of Satan operating all through history. It will end as it began with Satan trying to get the human race to bow down and worship him.

ROME VERSUS JERUSALEM

Consider several factors in favor of Rome rather than Jerusalem as the world headquarters, for the Antichrist and his church.

First of all, this world superman will need a big, impressive place ready to occupy when he comes to power. He doesn't have much time. In Revelation 4 the church goes to heaven. In chapter 5, the coronation of the King of kings gets underway. In chapter 6 the Antichrist makes his bid for power. The Bible says he will reign for 1,260 days. That's half of the seven-year period. Which half? I think he reigns for the first half because of the chronology of Revelation. And observe also that during the second half, the seven last plagues will be so completely devastating, as far as he is concerned, that things will be out of control. Perhaps that will set the stage for many nations like Israel, Russia and China to rebel. Read chapter 16 again and remember our previous message on the seven last plagues. Then imagine, if you can, how the Antichrist could reign in a situation of utter chaos like that.

To be sure, it will take some time to consolidate the whole earth under his domain, but he doesn't need all of it to start his reign. He starts with ten countries of the revived Roman Empire, and that could happen overnight. After that he expands his domain to include the whole world. The chronology and the context of Revelation suggest that he comes to power very quickly. The world is waiting for him right now. Political, social, and economic problems are fast approaching such catastrophic dilemmas that the western world is getting ready to embrace him the moment he appears. I think this will happen very shortly after we leave for heaven.

Famines, earthquakes, pestilences, wars, religious apostasy, moral degeneracy, lawlessness, racism, poverty, economic collapse, utter selfishness and rebellion against all authority including God—all these are working together right now in a manner unprecedented in history to produce the "perilous times" which will set the stage for the Antichrist to walk into the waiting arms of a world in chaos and despair.

I say all of this to say that this world ruler does not need three and one-half years to set up his kingdom. He may, indeed, use that time to consolidate it, but then the outpouring of the judgments of God will break it up. I think Russia will come into this world-kingdom after she is too weak to resist because of her defeat by supernatural intervention when she invades Israel early in the tribulation period (Ezek. 38 and 39).

Right now the world is moving from crisis to crisis and nothing seems to be settled permanently. Famine will stalk the earth, catastrophic developments in nature such as earthquakes, volcanoes, tornadoes and drastic changes in weather patterns will take place. Add to that run-away, worldwide inflation, accompanied by a collapse in the international monetary system and a severe worldwide depression—all of these I believe are not far ahead. They will all increase together, leading up to a great, climactic moment in history—the second coming of Christ.

Imagine how intense will be the feeling of people all over the world for world-government with a superman to take control. At that moment the greatest crisis of all will trigger the mad clamor for superman to take over. I'm talking about the moment when millions of people will suddenly disappear from the earth.

It is very likely that the truth concerning the rapture of the Christians by the power of God will be turned into a lie by the great deceiver, the author of lies, Satan.

Suppose he sends a demonic deluge of UFOs all over the earth and in the kingdom of men the rapture of the bride of Christ is explained as a wholesale kidnapping of mortals by beings from outer space. Think about that! What a crisis that would precipitate! Who can tell how it will happen?

A world emergency of great magnitude could result in immediate and willful recognition by mankind universally of a Supreme Ruler and Dictator of planet Earth. The Bible calls this man "Antichrist" and says that he will pretend to take the place of God. He will organize the world into one church and demand that he be worshiped as God.

You can see that he will need a world capital of awesome and impressive stature to befit the King of Earth and he will need it quickly. Yet he will not have time to build it since his total reign is only 1,260 days. So we ask: Is there such a place in existence? Yes, there is and here is the Biblical description, item by item.

FUTURE CAPITAL OF THE WORLD

1. It must be a city of seven hills (17:9)
2. It must be a great city (17:18 and 18:2, 10)
3. It must have access to the sea without being on the shore itself (18:17)
4. It must be a city of great wealth—gold, silver, tapestries, ivory, metals and marble (18:3, 11-17)
5. It must be a city that sits as a queen (18:7) and reigns over kings (17:18)
6. It must be a city without equal (18:18)
7. It must be a city displaying unusual craftsmanship (18:22)
8. It must be a city of many candles (18:23)
9. It must be a city responsible for spiritual fornication and murdering of many Christians (17:6)
10. It must be a city arrayed in purple and scarlet and decked with gold and jewels (17:4 and 18:16)
11. It must be a city that trafficked in the souls of men (18:13)
12. It must be a city of great sin (18:5)
13. It must be a city that lived in luxury ("lived deliciously") (18:7, 16)
14. It must be a city that causes one to stand in awe and marvel with great admiration (17:6)
15. It must be a city that can be *totally* destroyed without injury to Bible prophecy (18:8)

Now, is there such a place ready and waiting or must the Antichrist build it when he comes to power? The answer is: Yes, there is such a place! *Every detail fits.* That city is Rome, the heart of which is Vatican City with its Vatican museum and St. Peter's Basilica.

One must stand in awe as he enters St. Peter's, the largest, most magnificent cathedral in the world. It is 600 feet long and 400 feet wide. The Papal Altar is a magnificent work of art. Its four huge, twisted bronze columns hold the canopy overhead 75 feet above the floor of the church. The great dome overhead is 400 feet high.

With one exception, the pictures are all mosaics, not paintings. The statues are huge, abundant, impressive and irreplaceable. The most famous is the Pieta. The most prominent is that of Peter in black marble seated on his throne.

The last time I was there preparations were being made for a special holy day. It was Saturday night and they slipped a scarlet robe on Peter, put a crown full of dazzling jewels—diamonds, sapphires, rubies and emeralds—on his head and a huge ring with a large, rare, red ruby on his finger. All the while his feet were bare and his big toe was half worn away from the kisses and caresses of misguided worshipers hoping to gain favor with God.

The preserved bodies of two dead popes lie in lighted caskets in full display. They are dressed in purple and scarlet and decked with gold and jewels. People kneel to pray before them.

Indeed, this cathedral is awesome beyond words. Could such a place be built in a few years? No, indeed! The wealth of the continents of the world flowed into Rome for 400 years to build this incredible edifice. Words are not adequate. One must see it for himself. There is nothing like it in all the world. And one should also visit the famous Sistine Chapel, the Papal gardens, and the Vatican Museum—wealth beyond compare!

It is my conviction that this place is ready and waiting to be the capital of the world. There is nothing like it anywhere. The art and craftsmanship could not be duplicated today. No wonder John said that he stood in awe and wondered with great admiration (17:6).

Now I must hasten to say something to my Roman Catholic friends. Some of you are getting "mad" at me. Please note, I did *not* say that the Pope is the Antichrist. Furthermore, I will not say that.

If you are a saved Roman Catholic (that is, if you have been saved through faith in Jesus Christ), you will not be here when all this happens, so what do you care? If you are not saved, you should be listening with both ears wide open until you find out how to be saved. Otherwise you are headed for unspeakable experiences during the outpouring of the wrath of a Holy God upon a world bent on all-out rebellion against the Creator. Unless, of course, you die before the Antichrist comes to power, in which case you will be in worse trouble in the fires of hades.

Bible scholars may disagree as to when or where the Antichrist begins his reign. But one thing is certain: a man energized by Satan will rule the world after the Christians have gone to heaven. John calls him "the beast." He will order universal worship of himself and he will get it. Then the judgment of God will be poured out upon him and in due course he will be thrown into hell. We shall see this when we get to chapter 19.

Now notice verses 10 and 11 of the 17th chapter.

> And there are seven kings: five are fallen, and one is, and the other is not yet come; and when he cometh, he must continue a short space.
> And the beast that was, and is not, even he is the eighth, and is of the seven, and goeth into perdition.

The seven kings (or kingdoms) in my opinion, refer to *seven* world empires of history. Each reigned supreme for a time. Here they are: (1) Egypt; (2) Assyria; (3) Babylon; (4) Medo-Persia; (5) Greece; (6) Rome; (7) The Revived Roman Empire of ten nations; and (8) The One-World Empire of the Antichrist.

Note: John says that five are fallen and one is (now). John wrote in the first century A.D. The first five mentioned were already gone. The one which was in existence in John's day was number 6—Rome. So far it is easy. Then John says number 7 continues only a short time. That appears to be the Revived Roman Empire which is formed out of ten nations which come out of the old Roman Empire. This coalition lasts just long enough to put the Antichrist on the throne. He then expands his kingdom to include the whole earth. He is called "the beast" and is said to be number 8, but came out of number 7. In verse 17, we read that the ten kings will "give *their* kingdom unto the beast." So they have a kingdom, but only for a very short time.

That brings us to verses 12 and 13.

> And the ten horns which thou sawest are ten kings, which have received no kingdom as yet; but receive power as kings one hour with the beast.

These have one mind, and shall give their power and strength unto the beast.

In verse 3 we were told the beast had ten horns. Here we are told the meaning of those horns. They are ten kings (or kingdoms or countries) which were not in existence in John's day but will be in existence in the time of Antichrist. They will unite and serve as a power-base for the world ruler. The Biblical phrase "one hour" is used to indicate a very brief period of time. Incidentally, all this matches what Daniel tells us about the image with *ten toes*. It's the same story.

Any student of history will be fascinated by the unfolding drama of current world events which is fast setting the stage John described here nearly two thousand years ago.

A few years ago, after many centuries of warring with each other, some of the countries which were part of the old Roman Empire banded together in an economic organization known as the "Common Market." And, as of January 1981, they have exactly ten members. These ten will elevate one of their leaders to the absolute dictatorship of planet Earth.

RUSSIA WILL NEVER RULE THE WORLD

Nowhere in the Bible are we told the names of these ten countries, but according to the prophecies of Daniel 7:8, and others, they must come out of the old Roman Empire. That means Russia will never rule the world. The same goes for China. It cannot be! God's prophecies are clear on this. They have never failed and never will.

It is interesting to note that the late Dr. Louis Bauman, one of the greatest prophecy preachers of the first half of this century, used these prophecies to predict that Germany would be divided. The eastern half was not in the original Roman Empire, and Dr. Bauman made the prediction in the days of Hitler when it seemed most unreasonable. So today West Germany is in the European Common Market and East Germany is a satellite of Russia. That fits the Biblical requirement for the end-time.

Verse 14 in our text will become much clearer when we get

to the nineteenth chapter. The Antichrist will try to fight the Lord when He comes in mighty power as the King of kings and Lord of lords with all the redeemed saints. But there will be no contest. He, the omnipotent God, will cast *the beast* into the lake of eternal fire.

DESTRUCTION OF BABYLON

We are ready now for chapter 18 in which John describes the final judgment and destruction of the city which was the capital of the world and headquarters for the world church. I think it is destroyed by the devastating seventh plague when the cities of the earth fall. In verse 2 we read, ". . . Babylon the great is fallen. . . ."

Not only is the city reduced to rubble, but it is also set aflame. Ironically, it would appear that the political leaders that put the Antichrist in power are the ones who start the fire.

In 17:16 we read, "And the ten horns . . . shall . . . burn her with fire." "Her" refers to the woman on whose forehead is the name Babylon according to verse 5. So now Babylon is burning.

Why do these supporters of Antichrist set fire to the city? Perhaps because Antichrist has failed. In the face of the seven last plagues, he is helpless and can no longer claim to be God. Everybody now knows he is not God (Rev. 16:9, 11). But then, too, we read in 17:17 that God hath put it in their hearts to fulfill His will. God sometimes "makes the wrath of men to praise Him" as He uses evil men to punish other evil men.

Now read verse 4 of chapter 18.

And I heard another voice from heaven, saying, Come out of her, my people, that ye be not partakers of her sins, and that ye receive not of her plagues.

Inasmuch as the world church is already in the process of development, it is appropriate that God should give this warning to us. We are not to help build this "ecclesiastical octopus" which is even now growing rapidly all over the world and in many cases is trying to discredit and destroy true, evangelical Biblical churches.

And, of course, during the tribulation period, this instruction may be just the encouragement the new believers will need as they face the choice: Christ or Antichrist. They will choose Christ and pay with their lives. They become tribulation martyrs.

Now read verse 8:

> Therefore shall her plagues come in one day, death, and mourning, and famine; and she shall be utterly burned with fire: for strong is the Lord God who judgeth her.

It appears to me that God's fierce anger is poured out in such intense judgment that the whole city is set on fire in a single day. In verses 16-19, we are told the wealthy merchants watch from their ships and from the surrounding hillsides, as they weep and lament, saying,

> ... Alas, alas, that great city, that was clothed in fine linen, and purple, and scarlet, and decked with gold, and precious stones, and pearls!
>
> For in one hour so great riches is come to nought. And every shipmaster, and all the company in ships, and sailors, and as many as trade by sea, stood afar off,
>
> And cried when they saw the smoke of her burning, saying, What city is like unto this great city!
>
> And they cast dust on their heads, and cried, weeping and wailing, saying, Alas, alas, that great city, wherein were made rich all that had ships in the sea by reason of her costliness! for in one hour is she made desolate.

I strongly urge you to read chapters 17 and 18, verse by verse, and word by word. In the light of what I have just told you, let God speak from the pages—giving you deep spiritual understanding.

Remember back in chapter 6 we were told the martyrs, killed by Antichrist, cried to God to do something and avenge their blood. They cried for justice, "How long, O Lord!" And now at last God is answering their cry.

ALL HEAVEN REJOICES

At this point they are in heaven. The coronation of the King of kings has just been consummated. And at this point, all heaven is told to rejoice in the just judgment that God has poured upon the city of Antichrist and his church. This is final. God is going into action. His Christ will soon appear in the sky.

THE TRUE KING IS COMING!

The newly crowned King of kings, with His new bride, will come down out of the blue in mighty power. Every eye shall see Him, every knee shall bow, and every tongue shall confess that JESUS CHRIST IS LORD.

O, what a day! All His enemies will finally lick the dust and He will take possession of His property—the planet Earth—and He will reign "where e'er the sun doth his successive journey run."

The age of grace will be forever past and henceforth the King of Righteousness will reign—for 1,000 years on the earth and in the eternal state forever.

Hitler butchered and murdered six million Jews. Stalin murdered ten or twenty million people. Mao has the blood of thirty to fifty million human beings on the record against his soul.

And the Communists of Indo-China by blood baths, purges and evacuation of whole cities, have undoubtedly caused several millions of their people to die from torture, exposure and starvation. Somehow, it seems to us God is silent. And we cry, "How long, O Lord, How long?" But remember, friends, God will not be silent much longer. There is coming a day when God will intervene. His judgment will fall. And none shall escape. Sin will be judged, and punishment will follow.

Are you helping build the world church by lending your name, giving your money? If so, God says, "Come out of her . . . and be not partakers of her sins."

Or perhaps you aren't even saved. In that case, absolutely nothing in all the world is more important right now than to settle the matter of your own personal sin and guilt before a holy God. Most dictators of history were tryants and monsters of evil deeds. They will be punished.

But remember, my friend, the Bible tells us we are all sinners.

And therefore, even the best of us stands in need of a Saviour. The Bible says that Saviour is Christ. So I'm asking you now to humble yourself before God, bow your head, and ask Jesus to come into your heart. The Bible says, "Whosoever shall call upon the name of the Lord shall be saved."

LET US PRAY

Lord, help someone right now to pray the prayer of a sinner and say, "Lord Jesus, I'm a sinner. I acknowledge that I cannot save myself. You died in my place, and I believe it. So, therefore, I now accept you as my substitute. Come into my heart. Forgive my sins. Help me to live for you the rest of my life."

And Lord, I pray you'll give spiritual insight and determination in the power of the Holy Spirit to every believer to stand firm on the side of the Bible and the true church of Jesus Christ in these closing days of the age of grace. In Jesus' name, Amen!

VII

The Coming of the
King of Kings

REVELATION 19

We are about to view one of the most magnificent and spectacular scenes that mortals will ever see. The title of the book we are studying is: "The Revelation of Jesus Christ." Revelation means to reveal or unveil. The original Greek word is *Apocalypse* which, of course, means the same thing. The whole book is about the revelation of Jesus in mighty power to the whole universe. We've come through 18 chapters and now at last in chapter 19 we come to the climax—the unveiling of Christ.

The first five verses rehearse the story of the last message— the destruction of the headquarters of the world church that was worshiping Satan and killing the saints of the tribulation period. According to verse 4, angels and redeemed mortals ("elders") will glorify God by saying, "Amen; Alleluia." Alleluia is the Greek form of the Hebrew word "Hallelujah." In simple terms it simply means rejoice and give glory to God.

In verse 6 we have the great climactic heavenly announcement:

ALLELUIA . . .
THE LORD GOD OMNIPOTENT REIGNETH

Verses 1 through 6:

And after these things I heard a great voice of much people in heaven, saying, Alleluia; Salvation, and glory, and honour, and power, unto the Lord our God:

For true and righteous are his judgments: for he hath judged the great whore, which did corrupt the earth with her fornication, and hath avenged the blood of his servants at her hand.

And again they said, Alleluia, And her smoke rose up for ever and ever.

And the four and twenty elders and the four beasts fell down and worshipped God that sat on the throne, saying, Amen; Alleluia.

And a voice came out of the throne, saying, Praise our God, all ye his servants, and ye that fear him, both small and great.

And I heard as it were the voice of a great multitude, and as the voice of many waters, and as the voice of mighty thunderings, saying, Alleluia: for the Lord God omnipotent reigneth."

THE WEDDING

The next two verses tell the story of the wedding of Christ and his bride, the church. During the seven-year tribulation period on earth, three tremendous events take place in heaven: (1) The Rewarding of the Saints, (2) The Coronation of the King; and (3) The Wedding.

Verses 7-8:

> Let us be glad and rejoice, and give honour to him: for the marriage of the Lamb is come, and his wife hath made herself ready.
>
> And to her was granted that she should be arrayed in fine linen, clean and white: for the fine linen is the righteousness of saints.

The marriage is a mystery. We mortals cannot possibly comprehend all that is involved. We only know what God says and He says "the marriage of the Lamb is come." So there will be a wedding. This will be a wedding to end all weddings in the sense that it will be an extravaganza beyond human comprehension.

THE BRIDE'S GOWN

John saw the wedding and he records what he saw. Interestingly enough he seems awed by what the bride is wearing. In the description of the wedding, half of the account pertains to the wedding gown.

Even today people are impressed by what the bride wears to her wedding. In twelve years in the pastorate I had my share of weddings. One thing that always amazed me: no matter how homely the bride was the day before, when the organ played "Here Comes the Bride" and people looked toward the aisle, they always remarked, "Isn't she beautiful!" That wedding gown really does something for a bride. Even if she is beautiful without it, she is stunning with it.

Well, in a mysterious way that we cannot now comprehend, we are the bride of Christ. All true believers, saved between the cross and the rapture, constitute the church of Christ and as such make up "his body," the bride. And now at this point in our text we are to be exhalted and honored above measure as we are wed to Him. Imagine that!

So what will we wear? John leaves us far below as he soars into the heavens and describes the bride's apparel as being "fine linen, clean and white," which is "the righteousness of saints."

If John had talked about earthly linen, wool, silk, cotton,

nylon, orlon or dacron, I could understand, but "righteousness" as a fabric—that I must confess is way over my head—so to speak.

To find answers to Biblical problems, the best solution is to search the Scriptures. When we do this we discover that we have no righteousness of our own. The righteousness of the best of us is as "filthy rags" in God's sight. So what could all this mean?

We study further and we discover that when Christ took our sins away He in turn imputed (gave) to us His own righteousness.

> For he hath made him to be sin for us, who knew no sin; that we might be made the righteousness of God in him (II Cor. 5:21).

Marvelous wonder of wonders. By His shed blood in substitutionary atonement, He cleansed me from all sin and then to top it all He clothed me in His righteousness and declared me to be a saint . . . all because of His sacrifice, His love, His mercy, and His grace.

What can we say but: Praise God, Hallelujah! We are already clothed in the heavenly garments but to our earthly eyes they are invisible. When we exchange time for eternity and move to the celestial realm, we, as the redeemed bride of Christ will be wearing the most beautiful garments any eyes have ever seen— all made out of the righteousness of Christ.

They'll fit as perfectly as your skin and they will be totally comfortable. What's more, they'll never be soiled, they'll never grow old, and they'll never wear out. Spotless, sparkling, dazzling, brilliant white—robes of pure righteousness! No wonder John is spellbound. From the next verse I gather that as John gazes at the bride in all her beauty and splendor, he forgets to keep writing. Perhaps he is spellbound when he sees the bride. At any rate, we read in verse 9:

> And he saith unto me, Write, Blessed are they which are called unto the marriage supper of the Lamb. And he saith unto me, These are the true sayings of God.

Here below when we have a wedding, the ceremony is followed by the reception and then comes the honeymoon. When our daughter, Joan, found the man of her dreams, a wedding was arranged. What a happy and delightful occasion to see them both so happy and so wonderfully dedicated to the Lord.

Then there was a reception with food, fellowship and friends—dear friends. After that the "chariot" was waiting at the door to take them on their honeymoon. Off they went to live "happily ever after" as the saying goes. The fact that it turned out to be a Volkswagen didn't change their dreams.

So in heaven there will be a wedding followed by a feast and that will be followed by the honeymoon when the King will take His new bride to His kingdom to reign with her forever.

JOHN IS OVERWHELMED

Awestruck, spellbound, flabbergasted and speechless, John prostrates himself on the heavenly floor at the feet of an angel to worship him. He is quickly reprimanded and told to

WORSHIP GOD

In two words John is told an important and far-reaching truth that mortals all over the world ought to know and observe. Worship is reserved for God alone. Nobody and no thing is to be the object of our worship but God only. Not angels. Not the blessed, holy Virgin Mary. Not statues, not icons (pictures)—nothing! John, in his vision made this mistake; we in our glorified bodies will make no mistakes. So we'll never worship angels; you can be assured of that.

Verse 10:

> And I fell at his feet to worship him. And he said unto me, See thou do it not: I am thy fellow-servant, and of thy brethren that have the testimony of Jesus: worship God: for the testimony of Jesus is the spirit of prophecy.

The last line of that verse could be the text for the whole book. It says that Christ and prophecy are inseparably linked together. Anything said about Jesus or anything Jesus said invariably leads to prophecy. By the same token, when we start with prophecy, we inevitably come to Christ. Christ and things-to-come cannot be separated.

And now at last we are ready for the great day of God Almighty to appear in the clouds with power and great glory.

THE REVELATION OF JESUS CHRIST

For this moment the holy angels have waited ever since Adam and Eve ate the forbidden fruit and sin entered the human race. For this moment every follower of Christ was taught to pray:

Our Father which art in heaven,
Hallowed [holy] be thy name.
THY KINGDOM COME (Matt. 6:9-10).

Of this moment Enoch preached nearly 5,000 years ago (Jude 14): "Behold, the Lord cometh with ten thousands of his saints." And the prophet Zechariah, nearly 500 years before Christ, wrote ". . . the Lord my God shall come, and all the saints with thee" (Zech. 14:5). In verse 9, the prophet adds: "and the Lord shall be *king over all the earth:* in that day. . . ."

The King is coming, so look to the skies as we read in Revelation 19:11-13:

And I saw heaven opened, and behold a white horse; and he that sat upon him was called Faithful and True, and in righteousness he doth judge and make war.

His eyes were as a flame of fire, and on his head were many crowns; and he had a name written, that no man knew, but he himself.

And he was clothed with a vesture dipped in blood: and his name is called The Word of God.

The last time we saw heaven opened was in chapter 4, verse 1, when the bride went up. Now it is opened again and out comes the groom with His bride; they are going on their honeymoon.

A WHITE HORSE

He is not driving a white Cadillac; He is riding a white horse. Shall we take it literally? Well, John says he saw it. If you spiritualize the horse, explaining that it stands for war, you'll have a problem when we get to verse 14. So I take it just like John says he saw it.

A WARRIOR AND A JUDGE

Christ is indeed going to war. As the personification of faithfulness and truth, He now proceeds to fulfill His word and execute judgment in righteousness. With eyes like a "flame of fire" He comes as a warrior; He comes as a judge; He comes as a king.

Notice He does not come now as the lowly babe of Bethlehem. This time He will not permit evil men to put a purple robe on Him and mock His kingship. He will not now submit to scourging and torture. He will not now allow His enemies to drive spikes through His hands and feet and nail Him to the old rugged cross. Oh, no! That was the first time when He came to *die.* But this time He comes to *reign.*

In magnificent array, in mighty splendor, in omnipotent power He comes to take possession of His property—the planet Earth.

Ah, mortals! Earthlings! People of earth! Fall on your knees; bow down before Him! The King is coming! The prophets foretold of this day when they said *every* eye shall see Him; *every* knee shall bow and *every* tongue shall confess that JESUS CHRIST IS LORD.

The age of grace is forever past. Men will no longer be allowed to curse God and live. Today a man can stand up and curse God; he can use His name in vain in every other breath; he can look to the sky and blaspheme the name of the God of heaven; he can deny His very existence; he can even stand in the pulpit and blaspheme God and deny everything that is sacred; and yet God, in love and mercy, waits for him to repent and come and receive the salvation that is freely offered to "whosoever will." This is the age of grace when God waits in patience and in love and long-suffering and mercy for any wicked sinner to come back to Him. But one day, friend, that will all be over. One day it will be too late.

Let's return to our text. In verse 12 we are told He has many crowns. This indicates the many titles He bears, more than any earthly monarch. The Bible is full of them. Seed-of-the-woman,

Shiloh, Messiah, Jesus, Saviour, Lord, Wonderful, Counsellor, Everlasting Father, Prince of Peace, Son of man, Son of God, King of kings, and Lord of lords—all these and many more, are the titles He bears, indicated by the crowns He wears. Thus, there are many crowns.

But in the end of verse 12 we have a strange statement: ". . . he had a name written, that no man knew, but he himself."

I studied this verse for 25 years before I found an explanation that satisfies me. One day as I was meditating on this verse it suddenly dawned on me. I think the Lord gave me this understanding.

Of all the titles that are His, there is one that we will never be able to comprehend or understand. That is the title of deity—God!

Even though we, in our redeemed and glorified bodies stand by His side as His bride, elevated above all beings of all time—even above the holy angels—yet we will never be God. He is infinite; we are and always will be finite. It is impossible that finite beings could ever comprehend or know what it means to be God! That is one of His titles which nobody will ever be able to comprehend.

"THE WORD" IS CHRIST

In verse 13 we are told one of his names: The Word of God. John in his Gospel says:

Chapter 1, verse 14:

And the Word was made flesh, and dwelt among us, (and we beheld his glory, the glory as of the only begotten of the Father,) full of grace and truth.

There is no question about it. Christ is called "the Word." The Bible is the written word; when Christ speaks, it is the spoken word; but Christ in person is the Living Word. So there can be no doubt about the identity of the one to whom John refers in this chapter.

GARMENTS OF THE GROOM

We talked about the bride's wedding gown, but what does the groom wear? John says, ". . . he was clothed with a vesture dipped in blood. . . ."

To understand this, we must remember the grand, overall sweep of this whole book. Remember, He is coming to possess the property which He bought with His own blood. In chapter 5 we saw Him appear as the slain lamb who paid the purchase price not only for a lost human race, but also for a sin-cursed earth. So now when He comes to take possession, He comes wearing His receipt.

His garments are dyed with His own blood. Considering the occasion and the circumstances, I'm sure this is not a gruesome thing but rather, like the nailprints in His hands, a thing of great beauty. After all, He is altogether lovely! So His garments will be royal red. Think of the color scheme for the wedding—the bride in spotless, sparkling white; the groom in brilliant red.

What a magnificent sight! Allow the Holy Spirit to show you a glimpse of His Majesty dressed in crimson, riding on a heavenly white charger, coming down out of the blue, as the newly crowned King of kings, to reign on the throne of His father David.

HIS BRIDE ACCOMPANIES HIM

Verse 14:

And the armies which were in heaven followed him upon white horses, clothed in fine linen, white and clean.

Put verses 8 and 14 together and you know who is coming to reign with Him. After all, in chapter 5 when the redeemed bride in heaven sang the song of redemption at the coronation ceremony, these were some of the words: "And we shall reign on the earth." Now the time has come. The redeemed ones will reign with Christ.

So here comes the bride on her honeymoon, dressed in fine, heavenly linen, clean and white, made out of righteousness—perhaps a few hundred million strong—all driving new Lincoln

Continentals. Is that what it says? No, indeed! It says, "riding on white horses."

Somebody is asking, "Are you going to take that literally, too?"

So I ask, "How are you going to take it? What does it say?"

If your answer is that the horses here should be taken figuratively because they symbolize war, I will remind you very quickly that the bride is not going to war. I will be on one of those horses, but I will not be on my way to war.

A rule which I follow that works extremely well is this: Take the Bible literally, just like God wrote it, unless the Bible itself, mixed with a little common sense indicates otherwise. I'll show you how this works when we get to verse 15 where the sword is obviously figurative.

But here, I am satisfied, we'll have to take it just like John wrote it. Otherwise we have a problem: What was it John saw them riding? I have no problem here. I think John saw beautiful, lovely horses.

ANIMALS IN HEAVEN?

People often ask me, "Do you think there will be animals in heaven?"

My answer is, "Yes, indeed!" And to prove it I quote this verse. We will each have a pet horse. I hasten to remind you we don't need horses to travel in heaven. We will be in glorified bodies that are energized by pure spirit, able to move at will, in any direction, with the speed of thought. Think about that for a while.

When the rapture takes place and we rise to meet the Lord in the air, we will not have, nor will we need, any conveyance of any kind—no horses, no space ships, no flying saucers—nothing! Nothing but the pure power of the Almighty God—the Creator. That's all we'll need.

So why horses here in Revelation 19:14? The answer—just for pleasure! God doesn't tell us too much about heaven. But we know "the half has never yet been told" and the Bible says, "at thy right hand there are pleasures for evermore." God is our loving Heavenly Father who delights to please His children. I think He has a lot of fantastic surprises waiting for us when we arrive and in this passage He lets us in on one of the surprises—a beautiful, white, heavenly pet horse.

PEGASUS, THE FLYING HORSE

When I was a boy in school, I read the story of Pegasus—a horse that could fly. In the mythology of the Greek gods is the story of a beautiful horse owned by Zeus, the king of the gods. It was said that on rare occasions, lucky mortals would catch a fleeting glimpse of this rare, beautiful, white steed as he sailed high in the sky over Mt. Olympus. And once in a great while he might be seen feeding on the green slopes of that mountain.

As a farm boy who was used to riding a horse that didn't get more than a few feet off the ground, it was kind of fascinating, and somewhat stimulating, to think about a horse that could sail off through space. Of course, it was all dismissed as pure fantasy—just mythology. However, years later when I studied Revelation, I discovered there really are such horses, and I own one. They are not earthly horses, but heavenly horses.

If you like beautiful horses all this will please you. If you don't like horses—well, you'll like horses when you get to heaven. So don't worry about it now.

Right now somebody is wanting to know if there will be dogs and cats in heaven. The Bible does not say. No other animals are mentioned except horses.

But I do know that God loves variety. He never yet made two snowflakes exactly alike, or two trees, or two people, or two fingerprints. In every realm of His earthly creation, He made an endless variety. Visit the seashell "factory" in Florida and try to count how many kinds of seashells God made. And so it is in all of nature.

Therefore, I conclude that among the surprise pleasures God has waiting for us in heaven, are many heavenly pets. But I can't prove it. We'll just have to wait and see. Meanwhile, don't worry about what might or might not be in heaven because you know "there will be no disappointments in heaven."

Back to our text. Try to picture this glorious scene. The King of kings in all His glory and power is riding down out of the blue on the most beautiful white horse you could ever imagine. Millions of redeemed saints, all riding on heavenly white horses follow Him. He is dressed in red; the saints are dressed in white. What a magnificent display of divine splendor as the wedding party accompanied by all the holy angels comes down through space approaching the planet Earth. This would be a good time to read Matthew's graphic description of that great event.

Matthew 24:27-31:

> For as the lightning cometh out of the east, and shineth even unto the west; so shall also the coming of the Son of man be.
>
> For wheresoever the carcase is, there will the eagles be gathered together.
>
> Immediately after the tribulation of those days shall the sun be darkened, and the moon shall not give her light, and the stars shall fall from heaven, and the powers of the heavens shall be shaken:
>
> And then shall appear the sign of the Son of man in heaven: and then shall all the tribes of the earth mourn, and they shall see the Son of man coming in the clouds of heaven with power and great glory.
>
> And he shall send his angels with a great sound of a trumpet, and they shall gather together his elect from the four winds, from one end of heaven to the other.

Bear in mind that He is coming as a warrior and a judge to punish and destroy His enemies. So John tells us in Revelation 19:15 that He comes with a sword.

Verse 15:

> And out of his mouth goeth a sharp sword, that with it he should smite the nations: and he shall rule them with a rod of iron: and he treadeth the winepress of the fierceness and wrath of Almighty God.

THE SHARP SWORD

John says a sharp sword issues from His mouth. Shall we take it literally? Common sense and the Bible both indicate it is figurative. Anybody knows that Christ would not ride down out of the sky biting on a blade of steel held between His teeth.

And the Bible clearly tells us His Word is sharper than any two-edged sword. A blade of steel can separate a man's head from his shoulders, but the Word of God can separate the body from the soul.

Notice John says that He shall rule with a rod of iron and He treads the winepress in fierce anger. What does all this mean?

Remember, He died to redeem sinful men. But at this point in time, the human race as a whole, has rejected Him and turned to worship Satan. So He comes now to throw Satan out and destroy these wicked rebellious mortals. As I said before, the age of grace is now past, henceforth He will reign with a rod of iron. Instant death will be meted out to all who dare to disobey.

His judgment here is pictured as a winepress. This was a familiar scene in John's day. Even today, a winepress can be seen in the garden, near the empty tomb in Jerusalem. It is a big vat cut out of the solid rock. Grapes were dumped in and somebody then trampled them until the juice flowed into a pit at the one end. So the Lord will now deal with men on the earth who have become so unspeakably wicked.

Now look at verse 16:

> And he hath on his vesture and on his thigh a name written, KING OF KINGS AND LORD OF LORDS.

There you have it. Now you know who He is. There can be no doubt about it. Revelation 17:14 tells us the Lamb is the King. The emblem on His thigh bears His name—KING OF KINGS AND LORD OF LORDS.

Just think! He will be our Groom, our Lord, our Saviour, our King. We'll be so proud of Him and so in love with Him. After all, He is the most beautiful, the most wonderful, the most glorious being in the whole universe and at this point we are married to Him. Think of that!

THE BANQUET OF THE BUZZARDS

Verse 17 tells about the supper God will prepare for the birds.

> And I saw an angel standing in the sun; and he cried with a loud

voice, saying to all the fowls that fly in the midst of heaven, Come and gather yourselves together unto the supper of the great God . . . .

This is the great day of God Almighty referred to in Revelation 16:14 and 16 as the time of the battle that will take place in the valley of Armageddon with the armies of the whole world participating. Zechariah calls it "the day of the Lord" in 14:1 and in the next verse he says all nations will fight against Jerusalem.

According to Zechariah, these soldiers will have their flesh, their eyes and their tongues consumed away while they stand on their feet. At the same time the Lord will cause them to lose their minds and they'll start killing each other (Zech. 14:12-13).

In spite of all this Jerusalem will be captured temporarily so that God may intervene and prove to the stubborn, self-confident unbelieving Jews that they need Him. When it becomes clear to them that without God, all is lost, they will be ready to respond and God will go into action.

Zechariah says in the third verse of chapter 14, "Then shall the Lord go forth, and fight against those nations. . . ."

So in the midst of all this the King of kings with all the hosts of heaven approaches the earth and according to Zechariah 14:4 and 5, the Lord will "land" on top of the Mount of Olives. That's the last place His feet touched the earth when He went up at the ascension.

When His feet touch the Mount of Olives, a great geographical miracle will take place. It will split in two, leaving a great valley.

It will all happen when the Lord comes *with* His saints (v. 5). Notice how all these things fit together.

Now with that background, look again at Revelation 19:17. An angel is in the air, silhouetted against the sun, giving the call for vultures all over the earth to migrate to Israel. God has prepared a banquet for the buzzards. In verse 18 we are told what they will eat.

That ye may eat the flesh of kings, and the flesh of captains, and the flesh of mighty men, and the flesh of horses, and of them that sit on them, and the flesh of all men, both free and bond, both small and great.

FIGHTING ON HORSEBACK

Note carefully the words "flesh of horses." These soldiers will be fighting on horseback. It couldn't be that horses are used to symbolize tanks. How would the birds eat steel? In my study of Bible prophecies involving more than a quarter of a century, I have observed that God has a way of saying exactly what He means and then He fulfills His prophecies to the letter.

So we have a problem. Why would the armies of the world in a scientific era revive the cavalry and avoid modern weapons of war? We don't know all the answers, but maybe we have a clue in the story of the seventh plague. Remember the awful electrical storm coupled with earthquakes and devastating hail. It may be that after that plague the modern weapons of war will be so demolished as to be incapacitated. At least that's a possible explanation. God doesn't say why, He just says what. And on the basis of past performance, He can be fully trusted to keep His word precisely.

NO CLASSLESS SOCIETY

There is something else in that verse that is very interesting. There will be different classes of society, "free and bond, small and great." After many centuries of man's attempt to create utopia on earth in the form of a classless society, it can be observed here that it has not been achieved.

Now let's read verse 19 where we have the

BEGINNING OF THE END

And I saw the beast, and the kings of the earth, and their armies, gathered together to make war against him that sat on the horse, and against his army.

All the armies under the leadership of the Antichrist now join forces to fight against the Lord and His heavenly hosts as they descend out of the sky.

They have been fighting Israel and Israel has been losing.

Now the Lord comes to her rescue. As Zechariah said, "Then shall the Lord go forth and fight against those nations. . . ." So we want to know: how does it all come out?

Remember, as members of the bride of Christ, we will be in that vast, heavenly host following the King. All the armies of earth, plus the Antichrist, and the devil himself will be out to destroy us. Read again the last line of verse 19.

But I'm so glad to tell you when you're on the Lord's side, you have nothing to worry about. We know He is all powerful and we have the written account in advance to tell us of the outcome. Therefore, at that point we will not have one anxious moment. Read the next verse with me and you'll see why.

Verse 20:

> And the beast was taken, and with him the false prophet that wrought miracles before him, with which he deceived them that had received the mark of the beast, and them that worshipped his image. These both were cast alive into a lake of fire burning with brimstone.

THE FIRST OCCUPANTS OF HELL

There cannot be two kings. The true King has come; now the false king must go. Christ, the mighty conqueror, speaks the word and the Beast (that is, the Antichrist) and the False Prophet (that is, his helper called a second beast in Rev. 13) are instantly thrown into the lake of eternal fire. In the Greek, this place is called Gehenna and nobody ever gets out of that awful abode. In our next message we'll look in and see these two persons of the devil's trinity still there—a thousand years after they were thrown in. So as far as earth is concerned, these two satanic individuals were "put away" forever.

They are the first occupants of hell. As of now hell is being prepared for the devil and his angels, but it is still an empty place. There is nobody in it yet. When Jesus talked about the rich man who died and went to hell, he used the word "hades."

Hades is a place in the heart of the earth where all the lost of all ages go immediately at death. There they await the final judgment in space where they must appear to hear their sentence pronounced. They will then be cast into *Gehenna*—the final hell of the Bible. We'll explain all of this in the next message.

Our chapter has one more verse, and it is so final. Read it carefully.

Verse 21:

> And the remnant were slain with the sword of him that sat upon the horse, which sword proceeded out of his mouth: and all the fowls were filled with their flesh.

THE LAST BATTLE IS OVER

At this point not one soldier is left alive. The author of life itself speaks and every one who is still alive at this point drops dead on the battlefield. Nobody goes home from the battle of Armageddon. And there never will be another war. At long last, this old earth will have peace because the Prince of Peace has come and He will enforce peace.

At this point you ought to reread the entire chapter, trying to picture the whole unfolding drama. It's all part of the future history of the world. In our next message, we will see what happens to Satan.

LET US PRAY

Our Heavenly Father, we praise Thee for the privilege of gathering as a group of believers in Thy house, unafraid and unmolested, to study Thy Word together. We pray that it may long continue to be so. We see the sinister forces of Satan and evil all around, trying to destroy the liberty which we have here in this land. We pray that Thou shall rule and overrule the forces of evil, so that the proclamation of Thy Word may go forth in liberty.

We pray, our Father, that if there be any in the audience tonight who are in the bondage of sin, in the family of Satan, that the Holy Spirit may take hold of them and dip them in the blood of the Lamb, and bring them up whiter than the snow. Remove from their shoulders the burden of sin which is getting too heavy to bear, and set them free in the liberty which is Christ. "Ye shall know the truth, and the truth shall set you free." That is what Jesus said, and we praise Thee, our God, we have found it to be true.

We thank Thee that we are children of Thine; our names are written in heaven and we are on the way to the holy city. But, in the meantime, O Lord, our hearts go out to many who stubbornly resist the still, small voice of the Holy Spirit, refusing to acknowledge they are sinners in need of a Saviour. We pray that they may see their need and may acknowledge and receive Him, who alone can save from sin.

Lord, bless everyone in divine presence. Help us to long for that day when we shall see our Saviour face to face, and make us to thrill with the thought that someday when we have been wed to Him, we shall ride out of the blue, coming down upon this earth with the KING OF KINGS AND THE LORD OF LORDS! Then we shall reign with Him in a wonderful world with a perfect government and a lovely environment for 1,000 years. And in the eternal ages we shall live and reign with our wonderful Lord forever.

Make us to rejoice with anticipation as we long for that moment, which we believe is very near, when we shall rise to meet our Saviour in the sky, forever, to be with Him and forever to be like Him. We pray it in Jesus' name. Amen!

VIII

The Last

Judgment

REVELATION 20

The Great Tribulation is over. The devil's church has been destroyed. Her headquarters, the city of seven hills, lies in ashes. The Antichrist and his helper, called the False Prophet, are both in the lake of fire. The battle of Armageddon is finished. Every last soldier is a corpse on the battlefield. The vultures are picking their bones.

THE KING HAS COME TO SET UP HIS KINGDOM

His bride and all the holy angels are with Him. And there stands Lucifer—all alone. He cannot talk and he cannot move. The King has turned off his power and he is helpless. Listen now as John tells us about

THE BINDING OF SATAN

Verses 1-3:

> And I saw an angel come down from heaven, having the key of the bottomless pit and a great chain in his hand.
> And he laid hold on the dragon, that old serpent, which is the Devil, and Satan, and bound him a thousand years,
> And cast him into the bottomless pit, and shut him up, and set a seal upon him, that he should deceive the nations no more, till the thousand years should be fulfilled: and after that he must be loosed a little season.

An angel binds Satan and locks him up in the bottomless pit. Four of his names are used in the second verse, but his original name was Lucifer. In his original estate he was Angel Number One, "the exalted angel" of heaven. He was created perfect in beauty, but he became proud and he rebelled against God, so he had to be thrown out of heaven. According to Revelation 12:4, it would appear that one-third of all the angels of heaven chose to join the rebellion. They are today disembodied, fallen angels called demons. All of this is hard to understand, but the Bible says it, and I believe it.

All of these centuries Satan has been roaming the world seeking to influence people to rebel against God by tempting man to sin. But now, finally, he will be cast into hades for 1,000 years. Six times John emphasizes the length of this period, and I see no reason to change it. I am sure the period will be exactly

1,000 years in length like the Bible says.

The bottomless pit or "shaft of the abyss" is, I believe, a place called hades or hell, in the heart of the earth where the lost souls of all ages, in flame and torment, await the last judgment. This is in harmony with many Scriptures that deal with the subject.

THE BOTTOMLESS PIT

Could there be any such place as a literal bottomless pit? My conclusion is that the heart of the earth is the true bottomless pit. Going toward the center of the earth from any point is down. And when you reach the center, there is no further "down." The opposite is also true that any direction away from the center of the earth is up. Think about that!

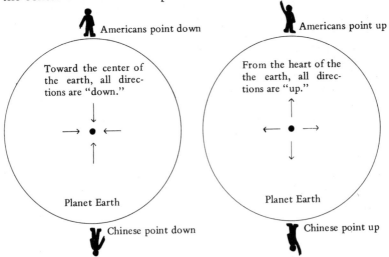

When I was preaching in the state of Kansas, the people told me about a bottomless lake. They said, "Would you like to see it?"

"Yes," I said, "that I would like to see."

When we got there, guess what! It was full of water. So how could a bottomless lake be full of water? Why didn't the water drop down to China? Or, more scientifically, why didn't it drop down a few miles and get changed to steam because of the intense heat? I was told the bottom of the lake connects with a shaft or underground passageway to the ocean. So the lake rises and falls with the ocean tide. That was very interesting, and it caused me to do some thinking—an exercise in which I engage occasionally.

At any rate, we are clearly told that Satan is imprisoned and for 1,000 wonderful years nobody can blame the old devil for his troubles. But at the end of the period, he will be let loose for a little while and I'll explain why later in this message.

The next topic John deals with is

THE FIRST RESURRECTION

Verses 4-6:

> And I saw thrones, and they sat upon them, and judgment was given unto them: and I saw the souls of them that were beheaded for the witness of Jesus, and for the word of God, and which had not worshipped the beast, neither his image, neither had received his mark upon their foreheads, or in their hands; and they lived and reigned with Christ a thousand years.
>
> But the rest of the dead lived not again until the thousand years were finished. This is the first resurrection.
>
> Blessed and holy is he that hath part in the first resurrection: on such the second death hath no power, but they shall be priests of God and of Christ, and shall reign with him a thousand years.

In the end of verse 5, John tells us what his subject is at this point. "This is the first resurrection," John says. So that is what he is talking about. The first sentence of verse 5 should be in parentheses. It's a bit of information John injects here, but explains in the latter part of the chapter.

Notice the two groups that have part in the first resurrection and who therefore reign with Christ. In verse 4 we clearly have the tribulation martyrs. Remember they were killed by the Antichrist for refusing to worship him. Of this group John says at the end of verse 4: ". . . *they* lived and reigned with Christ a thousand years."

But in verse 6 we are told all those who have part in the first resurrection will be priests of God and will reign with Christ for a thousand years. So who besides the tribulation martyrs would be referred to here?

To answer that we must refer to Revelation 5:10 where the redeemed ones in heaven are singing about how God made them His priests and how they will reign on the earth. Remember, this is in chapter 5 before the first seal is broken and therefore must be before there are any tribulation martyrs because the Antichrist does not appear until the breaking of the first seal which takes place after the choir sings.

The same group is referred to in I Corinthians 15:23. This is the great resurrection chapter of the Bible. Paul is telling us Christ is the first fruits of the resurrection and sometime later all those who belong to Him will be resurrected at His coming.

The harvest in Bible times is a symbol of what Paul is talking about. When the first grain ripened, God instructed the Israelites to sacrifice that first grain to Him and then He would guarantee the main harvest to follow.

So Christ is the first fruits of the resurrection because He rose from the dead to guarantee the "main crop" to follow. The "main crop" is that vast body of believers who will rise when the Lord comes in the air. So Paul says, ". . . afterward they that are Christ's at his coming."

Paul wrote to the Thessalonian Christians and told them, ". . . the dead in Christ shall rise first: then we which are alive and remain shall be caught up together . . . so shall we ever be with the Lord" (I Thess. 4:16-17).

So it is perfectly clear in Scripture that the great body of believers known as the church or the bride, will be the "main harvest" of the first resurrection, but the tribulation martyrs as the "gleanings" are included also in the group that will reign with Christ.

To summarize then: Both the tribulation martyrs and the believers during the Church Age, will have part in the first resurrection (1,000 years before the resurrection of the lost) and they will reign with Christ on the earth for 1,000 years.

THE FINAL REBELLION

Verse 7:

And when the thousand years are expired, Satan shall be loosed out of his prison.

The millennium has ended. By the way, we use that word even though it is not used in the Bible. It comes from a Latin word meaning "thousand," so it is a very good word to describe this period of 1,000 years.

But now it is over and Satan is about to be let loose. And, of course, we want to know why. The answer cannot be fully explained without giving a lot of details about the millennial reign. (For details on the millennial reign of Christ, a copy of the author's message on this subject is available on cassette tape.) But I'll summarize it sufficiently so you'll get the idea.

God always gives His creatures a choice to love Him or reject Him. This is true of angels and mortals. Some angels and all mortals chose to rebel. To mortals He sent a savior because all human beings since Adam were born with a sinful nature. Angels, already in heaven, could say, "Yes, God, I choose you and I choose to stay here." But human beings are sinners and cannot live with God by choosing to remain as they are. They can choose, but if they choose God there must be some way to clean them up and make them fit to live in God's holy presence. So God sent a substitute to take our sin upon Himself. Thus, Christ, the sinless One, died in our place. Now God can declare the penalty for our sin paid in full and judicially we are declared sinless in Christ.

For countless centuries God has given every mortal a choice: God or Satan—life or death—heaven or hell! As a race, man has continually made the wrong choice. The result has been that Satan is the god of this world.

His satanic majesty runs this world's system. Hence we have pride, greed, selfishness, jealousy, cruelty, suffering, wars, and all kinds of crimes from robbery to rape to murder. Throughout all history the world has experienced these things. And all these will get worse and worse as the end of this age approaches.

God is getting sick and tired of man's willful, wicked rebellion. So He is going to do something about it, and He has told us in great detail what He is going to do.

A PERFECT GOVERNMENT

He is going to send His Son the second time to earth. This time He will reign as King over all the earth. He will reign "in righteousness" "with a rod of iron." No outward acts of sin will be allowed under penalty of instant death. This old earth will finally have that which man could never achieve for himself—A PERFECT GOVERNMENT. Jerusalem will be the capital of the world; Israel will be the leading nation and Christ will be the absolute monarch of earth. There will be no more war and all crime will be abolished.

A LOVELY ENVIRONMENT

What's more, God will restore this planet to the paradise it was before the flood of Noah. He will clean up all pollution and settle that problem permanently. The climate all over the world will be delightful. Sickness and suffering will be almost non-existent. Death will be rare, except as the penalty of instant justice. Men and animals will again be herbivorous and people will live to be as old as trees. I didn't make all this up. If I had time, I could show you the Scripture to prove every item.

NO REAL CHOICE

So you see, it will be utopia on earth at last. But during this wonderful period, people will not really have a choice. They will be forced to "be good" even to the extent of being forced to gather regularly for the worship of Jehovah—whether they want to or not.

But finally at the end of the period, God will give every one a choice. This is how He does it.

SATAN IS LET LOOSE

We already read verse 7. Let's go on now with verses 8 and 9 to see what happens when the devil gets loose.

> And shall go out to deceive the nations which are in the four quarters of the earth, Gog and Magog, to gather them together to battle: the number of whom is as the sand of the sea.
>
> And they went up on the breadth of the earth, and compassed

the camp of the saints about, and the beloved city: and fire came down from God out of heaven, and devoured them.

Since he is the great deceiver, the father of lies, we are not surprised to discover that the first thing he does is to practice deception. This is where he left off a thousand years ago. And he covers the four quarters of the earth. In the Bible that means north, south, east and west.

Does he get any recruits? Amazingly enough, he gets so many, especially from Russia and her satellites, John cannot count the vast multitude.

One would imagine that the inhabitants upon seeing Lucifer would exclaim, "Lucifer, what are you doing here? We read all about how you brought sin and suffering with agony, heartache, poverty, crime, and death to the human race for so long. Now without you around, we have had a great time. Everybody is healthy and wealthy. We have lived in paradise for a thousand years. Now, Lucifer, we don't want you coming around and ruining it all; Lucifer, get out of here!"

Well, that's not what they will say. Judging by the reception the old devil is given, I can imagine they will say to him, "O Lucifer, we are so glad to see you. We are sick and tired of being 'good.' We want to do as we please. But we have had no choice. We have had no leader. Now, Lucifer, lead us. Let's go to Jerusalem and overthrow the administration of Jesus and His saints. Then we can do as we please."

TO JERUSALEM THEY GO

But the prophet Isaiah, promises there will be no more war. God will not allow it. When the army of Satan approaches Jerusalem, the Holy City, God will simply send a deluge of fire out of the sky and not one of them is left alive.

I think Satan has gathered every unsaved person on earth. People have made their choice, showing their real colors. During the millennium they were good outwardly, but inside they were as sinful as ever.

The purpose of this period is to show the human race once

and for all eternity that a perfect government and a lovely environment are not enough to change the sinful heart of man. It takes a new birth.

THE END OF TIME

So now every unsaved person on earth is dead. They died in the fire and have gone to hades which at this point "contains" every lost person who ever lived on the earth. There will never be any more sin. This is the end of time—the end of the world—literally.

SATAN'S DOOM

In verse 10 we read that Satan is cast into the lake of fire to join the other two members of the satanic trinity, the Antichrist and the False Prophet. They have been there during the entire 1,000 years, and they are still there when Satan joins them. Their torment will continue for an endless eternity. Nobody ever gets out of the lake of fire. Read it.

Verse 10:

> And the devil that deceived them was cast into the lake of fire and brimstone, where the beast and the false prophet are, and shall be tormented day and night for ever and ever.

The satanic trinity is in hell—probably somewhere on the rim of space in a place of eternal, black fire. These three are the only ones there at the end of verse 10.

All the lost of all ages are now dead and in hades in the heart of the earth. In the rest of this chapter, John tells us how they are evacuated from hades in what he describes, in verse 5, as the resurrection at the end of the thousand years.

It's a sad, sad story which God has here recorded. All the lost of all ages will be thrown into Gehenna—the final hell of the Bible, to suffer torment with the devil and his angels forever and ever. This is the story of

THE LAST JUDGMENT

Verse 11:

> And I saw a great white throne, and him that sat on it, from

whose face the earth and the heaven fled away; and there was found no place for them.

God is silent concerning the saved ones of the millennium. I'm sure there are many, but God has not chosen to say anything about them or their evacuation from the earth. Nevertheless, I'm sure that's what happens. There have always been those who made the right choice and I'm sure many will sincerely worship the Lord and be saved during this period. Because in the eternal state, all the righteous will live with God in heaven, I'm sure the righteous ones out of the millennium will be there, too.

But let's talk now about the things John tells us in the eleventh verse.

THE GREAT WHITE THRONE

Somewhere a great white throne is set up. It can't be on earth; it's fleeing away. It can't be in heaven; the defendants at this judgment will never get inside the gates of pearl. So it must be in space, somewhere between earth and heaven.

Now look at the judge who occupies this throne. His face is stern. Even the earth and its atmosphere can't bear to witness the awful scene about to take place. But who could this judge be?

THE JUDGE ON THE THRONE

There is no doubt about it. None at all. The next verse tells us it is God. But which person of the Godhead? John 5:22 and 27 will settle that very definitely.

For the Father judgeth no man, but hath committed all judgment unto the Son;

And hath given him authority to execute judgment also, because he is the Son of man.

CHRIST IS THE JUDGE

Did you see what it says? *All* judgment is given to the Son. Put these two verses together and you have proof of two things: (1) The Son (Jesus Christ) is God; and (2) Jesus, as God, is the judge at the last judgment. I see no room for argument. It is settled. God's Word records it. You can't deny it is there. You can deny its truth. But in that case you'll have to find out the hard way, as one sad day you stand in that number before the Judge seated in the great white throne.

SAVIOUR OR JUDGE — WHICH?

Sometime, somewhere you will face Christ. You can face Him now and call Him Saviour or you'll face Him then and call Him Judge. Now there is still time. It's the Age of Grace; you have a choice. In that day it will be too late. You will have made your choice and it will be too late—too late.

Verses 12-13:

> And I saw the dead, small and great, stand before God; and the books were opened: and another book was opened, which is the book of life: and the dead were judged out of those things which were written in the books, according to their works.
>
> And the sea gave up the dead which were in it; and death and hell delivered up the dead which were in them: and they were judged every man according to their works.

THE JUDGMENT OF THE LOST

All the lost of all ages are now made to stand before the Judge of the universe to hear their sentence pronounced. I know the saved ones will not be there because of what God says in John 5:24. The saved ones have already passed from death unto life, and shall not come into judgment (condemnation).

There are many verses that indicate the same thing and the whole story of the Book of Revelation keeps us informed as to where the saved ones are. One thing is certain. They are not in this group to be judged.

GOD KEEPS BOOKS

Observe, there are many books containing all the works of the people gathered here. And according to the end of verse 12 and also verse 13, every last person here will be judged on the basis of his *works*.

Now that settles it! Everyone of these individuals is lost because Paul says, ". . . by the *works* of the law shall no flesh be justified" (Gal. 2:16). We can only be saved by the finished work of Christ on the cross of Calvary. It is impossible for any man to be saved on the basis of his own works; so I repeat: every person at this judgment is lost. And it's too late now to change.

THE BOOK OF LIFE

So what about *the book*? A single book all by itself is opened and John tells us it is the Book of Life. This book is the record of all the people who made a reservation for a mansion in the sky. You might call it the Register of Heaven. It contains all the names of all the saved of all ages. It's the total, complete, accurate and final list of all the people who ever lived who will spend eternity with God in the eternal state. It is opened here only for the purpose of showing these people that their names are not there. They made no reservation for heaven.

Hell has no register, but all those who failed to register for heaven will be cast into the only other place in the eternal state—namely, hell—which was prepared for the devil and his angels.

GOD'S BOOKS

What kind of "books" does God keep? We know the contents but not the nature of them. You can be sure God does not have a lot of angelic secretaries taking down everything you do in some kind of heavenly shorthand. God does not write on paper. All those ideas come from man on earth.

Let us suggest some possibilities. A lady had an operation on her brain. The surgeons opened her skull and attached tiny electrodes to various portions of her brain. Then they turned on a tiny current. When it was all over, this lady reported that during her operation, she relived her wedding day just as vividly as when it happened. Details she had long since forgotten came clearly to her mind.

Is it possible that the "books" God keeps on each person are really inside His head? Scientists tell us that everything we ever experienced in word, thought, or deed is all recorded in the mysterious and fabulous tape-recorder of the mind. It's unbelievable but true that you never exhaust the supply of "tape." You may be as smart as Einstein and live as long as Methuselah, yet you can never fill the automatic tape recorder of the mind.

When the lost of all ages stand before the Judge of the universe, maybe God will "turn up the current" and in a moment of time each person will relive his whole life's experience from cradle to the grave. Every thought, every word, every sight, every deed—they will all be included.

From such a record men will recoil in horror. But there will be no way to deny or destroy the record and there will be no place to hide. There was a time when the record could have been erased, but it's too late now. It reminds us somewhat of Watergate but, of course, this is infinitely more serious. The eternal doom and destiny of multiplied millions of mortals is about to be announced.

There is another kind of bookkeeping God might use. Scientists tell us that all sound, all sight and all thought are made up of tiny electrical impulses that travel along with different wavelengths.

One wavelength is recorded by the ear and we call it sound. Another is recorded by the eye, and we call it sight. Yet a third is recorded by a machine and we call it thought.

We are told that theoretically these electrical impulses move out from the point of origin and travel on indefinitely into space. So if we could somehow exceed the speed of light and be transported far enough into space—and if we could then capture those wavelengths, we could look back to planet Earth and watch ourselves being born. And we could each see and hear everything we ever did in our entire lives.

CALL HIM CORNSTALK

For example, from just beyond the north star I could watch a baby boy being born in a farmhouse in Pennsylvania. I could watch his sister, Leah, standing at the kitchen window staring at a field of corn. Then I could see her dash excitedly into the bedroom and announce to her mother, "Let's call him 'Corn-stalk.' "

I could hear his mother turn down that suggestion. Then I could hear a second suggestion, "Well, then, let's call him 'Jesus.' " But his mother turned that down, too, with the statement "We'll call him 'Nathan.' " And I did not know until just before my mother died a few years ago, she had prayed before my birth that I might be a preacher. For the first thirty years of my life, it must have been discouraging to my mother to see no signs of the answer to her prayer. The full story of how the Lord suddenly answered that prayer is recorded in my message on "The Devil's Church."

Back to our story of God's record keeping. I have suggested several possibilities of how God might do it. I don't know exactly what God's books are, but one thing I know: any person who does not accept Christ as Saviour in this life will face his whole rotten record some day at the great white throne. By the same token, I am happy to tell you that when a person confesses his sin to Christ and receives Him as personal Saviour, his record is wiped clean.

The Bible is clear. Our sins are "buried in the deepest sea" to be "remembered against us no more." Isn't that good news! It's all possible because in a spiritual sense we have been washed in the blood of the Lamb. It is the shed blood of Christ that atoned for our sin and without the shedding of blood there is no remission. How we ought to love Him and desire above all else to please Him!

You don't need to understand it, but you certainly must believe it to avoid the scene we have in this chapter.

Now look at the last two verses.

Verses 14-15:

And death and hell were cast into the lake of fire. This is the second death.

And whosoever was not found written in the book of life was cast into the lake of fire.

All the people who appear before the Judge will now be

thrown headlong, pell-mell into the open, belching mouth of a devil's hell. It's called the lake of fire.

Death and hades (hell) in verse 14 are abolished as these are cast in Gehenna, too.

Oh, the weeping and the wailing as the lost are told of their fate. What a horrible, horrible scene! Remember, I didn't write it; I'm just God's reporter. I've told you what God says. You can take it or reject it—now. But when you close your eyes in death, it will be forever too late to change your reservation.

The song says: "O my loving brother, when the world's on fire, don't you want God's bosom to be your pillow? Hide me, over in the Rock of Ages, Rock of Ages, cleft for me."

Christ is that Rock, and He alone can save you from the second death—which is eternal separation from God in the lake of fire.

LIFE AND DEATH

Life in the Bible refers to the joyful, happy existence we'll have in heaven. *Death* refers to the existence of lost souls in the torments of hell. It is not annihilation. There is no such thing as annihilation of the soul. Death is separation. *Physical death* is the separation of the spirit-soul from the body. When God, who is the author of life, gives the order for the soul to leave the body, physical death occurs—not before.

Spiritual death is separation of the individual from God. And since there are only two places in eternity and God is in only one of these places (heaven), that leaves the other one (hell) as the eternal abode of the lost—separated forever in an utterly lonely place of black fire in outer darkness.

Jesus was no liar. He said, "These shall go away into *everlasting punishment*." That's nothing to scoff at or argue about. If you deny it, it is your word against the word of Jesus. For myself, I'll take Jesus.

If you have not already done so, why not ask Jesus to save you right now. What have you got to lose? If you accept Him as your personal Saviour, He promises to wipe the record clean—

yes, whiter than snow. Furthermore, He promises to give you the gift of eternal life. With this course of action, you cannot lose. To reject Him is to lose everything.

God is waiting for your answer. What will your answer be?

LET US PRAY

O Lord, there are so many precious people headed for eternal separation from Thyself. Help us as Christians, somehow, to reach them with the good news: Jesus saves.

We confess that in us is no good thing. In ourselves, we are unlovely and unworthy. But we praise and thank Thee that while we were yet sinners, Christ died for us. We thank Thee that in the power of the Holy Spirit we accepted Jesus as our Saviour. Now help us, each one, to live for Him until He comes again.

And Lord, save somebody right now who feels the convicting power of the Holy Spirit tugging at his heart's door. Let him catch a glimpse of that awful scene when the lost will be cast into hell. Let him hear just a bit of the weeping and wailing of the judgment day.

Then cause him to rush quickly into Your loving arms as he receives You into his heart by faith. Then, Lord, give him the forgiveness of sin and the gift of eternal life. Give such peace and joy as alone can come to those who rest in Thee. In Jesus' name we pray. Amen!

IX

The
Eternal State

REVELATION 21 and 22

Everyone wants to go to heaven, but nobody wants to die. Perhaps if we learn more about this wonderful place we will fear less the gateway by which the saved person enters this celestial realm.

On one occasion after I preached about heaven, a lovely Christian girl of about 17, said to me, "I just can't wait till I die so I can go to heaven." That's a wonderful attitude, but I am delighted to inform you that every living Christian has an excellent chance of going to heaven without passing through the valley of the shadow.

THE LAST TWO CHAPTERS OF THE BIBLE

Now, let's talk about *heaven,* the eternal state of the redeemed. The Bible is divided into 1,189 chapters. Revelation 21 and 22 are the last two chapters in this book, and they contain the most complete, detailed description of heaven to be found in the entire Bible.

God is the only authoritative source of information we have about heaven. He alone knows all about this place. Apart from Him nobody knows anything at all about it. Therefore, we are extremely blessed in that God has, by divine inspiration, recorded in His Word exactly what He wants us to know.

But I must caution you. Heaven is so absolutely wonderful that even after we have read God's description, we won't know much about it unless we allow the Holy Spirit to be our illuminator. Paul wrote to the church in Corinth:

> . . . Eye hath not seen, nor ear heard, neither have entered into the heart of man, the things which God hath prepared for them that love him.
> But God hath revealed them unto us by his Spirit (I Cor. 2:9-10).

So then, let us attempt to empty our minds of mundane things and allow the indwelling Holy Spirit to do His work. To the extent that we do this, we will catch a glimpse of that glory world—the eternal state of the redeemed.

HEAVEN IS MORE THAN A CITY

I call it the eternal state because it is vastly more than a city.

Heaven indeed, is a city as we shall see, but it involves also a vast realm including the eternal earth. To illustrate: New York is a city, but it is also a large state. So, likewise, *The Eternal State.*

Look with me now at the first verse of Revelation 21 and let's see what God has to say. After all, that's what really counts. It doesn't matter what we think, but it does matter what God says.

A NEW EARTH

Verse 1:

> And I saw a new heaven and a new earth: for the first heaven and the first earth were passed away; and there was no more sea.

Remember, the devil and his angels and all the lost of all ages have been thrown into hell, the lake of eternal fire. We saw that in chapter 20.

Now John tells us he saw a new heaven (firmament) and a new earth. This is an astounding revelation. Of course, we want to know what happened to the old earth. We last saw it in verse 11 of the preceding chapter where it was empty and fleeing away from the Great White Throne Judgment taking place in space. It seems that John has skipped something because he moves so quickly from the empty, vacant old earth somewhere in space to a new, oceanless, glorified earth in the eternal state.

As we ponder this problem, we can almost hear John tell us "Brother Peter recorded that story in great detail. I am simply recording what the other writers did not. Put it all together, and you'll have the complete picture."

To find out then, what happened to the old planet Earth, we turn to II Peter 3:10-13. Read it thoughtfully.

THE OLD EARTH IS BURNED UP

Verses 10 through 13:

> But the day of the Lord will come as a thief in the night; in the which the heavens shall pass away with a great noise, and the elements will melt with fervent heat, the earth also and the works that are therein shall be burned up.

Seeing then that all these things shall be dissolved, what manner of persons ought ye to be in all holy conversation and godliness,

Looking for and hasting unto the coming of the day of God, wherein the heavens being on fire shall be dissolved, and the elements shall melt with fervent heat?

Nevertheless we, according to his promise, look for new heavens and a new earth, wherein dwelleth righteousness.

What a passage of Scripture! What a revelation! It says the old earth, along with the atmosphere, is *burned up*. Imagine that! Notice the reference to heaven here.

THREE HEAVENS

There are exactly three heavens in the Bible, no more, no less. Mythology has seven, but the Bible has three: (1) the atmospheric heaven—the home of the birds; (2) the astronomical heaven—the home of the stars; and (3) the celestial heaven—the home of God. The context usually indicates which one the Bible writer had in mind; so this is no problem.

Paul, in writing about the time he was stoned and left for dead, says that he was caught up into the third heaven. He was in God's home. But he "closes up" very quickly and simply informs us that he cannot talk about it.

Now read the first verse of Revelation 21 again and ask the Holy Spirit to make it plain to your mind and heart.

The old earth and the blanket of air around it went up in flame and exploded with a great noise. From the language Peter uses, it is clear to me that God "lets go" and all the atoms explode so that this earth and the air around it become one gigantic atomic bomb resulting in the most awful explosion you could ever imagine.

I have a complete message on "The End of the World," and I don't have time to go into detail on that subject now. Suffice it to say: nothing is annihilated. God made the elements out of atoms. Atoms are "particles" of energy in motion. The Creator simply returns the materials of this earth back to the energy (His power) from which He made them in the first place. Then out of that same energy He fashions a new earth with a new sky. That's what it says. For God who is the Creator, this is no problem at all. He will simply speak the word and it will be done—just like the first time.

ETERNITY AT LAST

At this point, eternity has dawned. Every sinner has been cast into hell and every vestige of sin has been forever removed. The old earth has been burned up and now there is a new, wonderful, glorified, eternal earth IN THE ETERNAL STATE.

Did you notice Peter's reference to "a new earth, wherein dwelleth righteousness"?

In this present age, righteousness *suffers*: in the millennial reign of Christ, righteousness will *reign*; but in the eternal state, righteousness will *dwell*. Isn't that beautiful!

As we read on, we discover there is also a city. John saw them both—the earth and the city.

THE HOLY CITY

Verse 2:

And I John saw the holy city, new Jerusalem, coming down from God out of heaven, prepared as a bride adorned for her husband.

The city has a special significance for the bride who is married to the King. We'll see that relationship again in verses 9 and 10. The bride and the city go together. But that's not hard to understand. The city is the headquarters of the King and certainly the bride will always be very close to the groom.

GOD WILL DWELL WITH MEN

Verse 3:

And I heard a great voice out of heaven saying, Behold, the tabernacle of God is with men, and he will dwell with them, and they shall be his people, and God himself shall be with them, and be their God.

The word tabernacle used here means dwelling place. So the saved people of all ages will dwell with God in the Eternal State. There will be an earth and there will be a city. Both will be in the celestial realm called heaven. There will be no division of abode. Everybody will live with God and He with them. Remember, at this point we are talking only of the saved people.

Now read one tremendous verse—verse 4—which tells us about things that will *not* be in heaven.

> And God shall wipe away all tears from their eyes; and there shall
> be no more death, neither sorrow, nor crying, neither shall there be
> any more pain: for the former things are passed away.

Heaven will be a wonderful place because of (1) the things that *will not* be there and (2) the things that *will* be there. Let's talk about the things that will not be in heaven.

NO TEARS

There will be no tears and no crying in heaven. Think about that. It should make you so happy that you want to cry. But that's because you are still in your earthly bodies and these earthly bodies are very much a part of this world.

Do you realize that tears are a gift from God to us who live in this "veil of tears." God knew exactly what He was doing when He created our bodies to be equipped with tear ducts. Tear ducts are

THE EMERGENCY VALVES OF THE SOUL

As long as we have problems and difficulties, sorrows and heartaches, death and pain, we need to be able to cry. That keeps us from "cracking up." When a loved one passes away and our hearts are so filled with sorrow that we think we cannot stand it, suddenly the emergency valves open and we have a good cry. That way the pressure is relieved and we feel better.

Years ago my uncle had a hot water tank in the basement of his Pennsylvania Dutch farmhouse. It was operated with gas. One time the steam pressure inside the tank built up so high that it exploded. There was no emergency valve. So the bottom of the tank blew out and the tank started up like a rocket. It went through the ceiling of the living room and into my grandmother's bedroom. It smashed a box full of her antique dishes as it continued upward. It went right through her bedroom ceiling and into the attic. If the rafters of the roof of that old house had been as flimsy as they are in some of the new houses which are being built today, who knows—that tank might have gone into orbit. You can be sure that when that tank was replaced it had an emergency valve on it.

So our earthly bodies need "emergency valves" but our heavenly bodies will need no such thing. We will never cry in heaven—not even at the beginning. The reference to God wiping away all tears leads some people to think we are going to start the reception in heaven by having a Kleenex party. They think everybody will be crying as hard as they can because of failures while back on earth; God will pass around the tissue and when they are all "cried out," so to speak, then the happy part will start.

I do not believe that sorrow can enter that perfect place and neither can tears. The Greek arrangement of the words referred to is simply their way of saying that God will abolish all tears; there will be no crying in heaven. The angels won't cry and neither will we.

By the way, tears here below are sometimes the result of the overflow of happiness. We may be so sad we can't stand it, or we may be so glad we can't stand it. In either case, we cry, and that brings relief.

For example, one can never tell about the tears at a wedding. Does the bride's mother cry because she is so sad she is losing a daughter, or because she is so happy she is gaining a son? In any case, the overflow of intense emotion necessitates tear ducts as long as we are in our mortal bodies here on this earth.

In heaven we will have no sorrow, but we will have overwhelming joy. But in that fair land, when we get so happy we think we can't stand it, we'll worship. John did it at the heavenly wedding, and we will do it endlessly as we live in a state of ecstasy throughout eternity in the land where there will be no more tears.

Heaven will also be a place where there will be

NO DEATH

Meditate on that for a while. From the moment we were born to this present time, we have been in a struggle with death. And unless the Lord returns first, death will be the victor in this conflict. Praise God—for the Christian it is only a temporary victory. The final victory will be ours because of Christ.

Try to imagine how wonderful heaven will be because there will be no more death. That means no more separation. No matter if you are a hard-nosed atheist, when you stand by the casket of a precious loved one, you must stand alone in silence and sorrow in the presence of the last enemy—death. And you are totally helpless to do anything about it.

Of course, the Christian knows that such separation is only for a little while and then "we shall meet again." That's why Paul wrote to the Thessalonian Christians encouraging them at the death of their loved ones, not to sorrow as others "which have no hope." Read it for yourself in I Thessalonians 4:13-14. The saddest experience in this world is to stand at the casket of an unsaved loved one and to know that there is no hope and we'll never, never meet again.

By contrast, to stand at the casket of a saved loved one even though it may be heartbreaking, one feels his sorrow mellowed with hope because he knows the separation is temporary and then will come the glad reunion on the resurrection morning when we'll never, never part again. O, what a contrast!

NO FUNERALS

Because there will be no death, there will be no funerals. And, of course, there will be no funeral parlors, no morticians, no cemeteries, no tombstones. By the same token, there will be no sickness and, therefore, no hospitals, no drugs, no doctors, and no nurses. We thank God for all of these now, but praise God there will be none of these in heaven. We won't need them. All the saved doctors and nurses will change their profession from medicine to music. The sounds familiar to them now will change to their very opposites. Moaning will change to mirth and lamenting to laughter.

NO FATIGUE

Because there will be *no* death, not even a cell in your heavenly body can die. That means there will be no fatigue. Most of you are tired right now. You've worked hard all day, you hurried to get to the services on time. And even though you are glad you are here, you are tired. Right? Right!

I want you to know that I appreciate the sacrifice you have been making to come out night after night. And if it is any consolation to you, I must tell you that when I get through preaching, I feel tired, too. As a rule, I do not feel it while I'm delivering the message God has given me. He not only supplies the message, but He also energizes His servants to do the job He assigns.

Traveling many miles, pouring out one's heart with a message from God to dying mortals—day after day, night after night, week after week, year after year—all this takes its toll. The spirit is willing, but the flesh is weak. So the cells die faster than the body can replace them and fatigue and old age set in. Suddenly, everybody in this audience is feeling tired and old.

Well, cheer up. I have good news. We are on the way to a place where you'll never feel tired again. There will be no tired people in heaven.

THE PLACE OF ETERNAL REST

Heaven is a place of eternal rest, but don't misunderstand. Heaven is not an old folk's home where all the tired, overworked people from planet Earth are sitting around in Kennedy rocking chairs, recuperating from all their terrestrial toil. No, indeed! The place of eternal rest is not a quiet, morbid place like a cemetery, but rather a place where everybody will be

ETERNALLY RESTED

It's like having your batteries fully charged all the time and knowing that they can never run down. In heaven we will be fully rested perpetually. It will be impossible to grow weary. No one will ever be tired. Fatigue will be totally abolished.

Part of the explanation lies in the fact that these earthly bodies are energized by blood which gets its energy from the food which God grows miraculously from the ground for our nourishment. On the other hand, our heavenly bodies will not have any blood. Flesh and bone, yes, but no blood. That's heavenly flesh and bone.

Our present bodies are mortal (subject to death); our eternal bodies will be immortal (not subject to death). So these present bodies will die; our heavenly bodies cannot. Furthermore, our heavenly bodies will be energized by *pure spirit.* We will be able to move at will in any direction with the speed of thought and we will never feel the slightest fatigue.

Because of all this we'll never grow old. How do you like that? Imagine a body that is wonderfully beautiful, eternally young, always fully charged with unlimited energy, can never grow tired and can never die.

If some chemist would invent a "pill" that people could swallow right now to achieve all these things, everybody on earth would give everything he had for such a magic potion.

Yet, when all this is offered free there are few takers. This can only be explained by the reality of our sinful natures and the activity of Satan in the spiritual realm.

To all that has been said we can add another wonderful fact. Heaven will be wonderful because there will be no more pain.

NO PAIN

Did you ever stop to think what a blessing pain is—that is, while we are in these mortal bodies? Pain is an urgent message from some part of the body signaling trouble and demanding a solution.

If you had a cavity that was destroying a tooth and there was no such thing as a toothache, the bacteria in that tooth could work unhindered, pouring poison into the bloodstream—even to the point of killing you and nobody would have known that there was anything wrong. See what I mean?

Some internal pain develops and the doctors go to work to find the trouble. Perhaps they decide it is appendicitis and they perform an appendectomy and your life is spared. So it goes. Pain serves a very useful purpose here on earth.

Unfortunately, a large majority of this audience has a pain right now if you stop to think about it. I guess it's mean of me to remind you—especially since I am not suffering from any aches or pains, myself. Colds, constipation, headaches, and so forth, are almost unknown to me and I do not average one aspirin a year. I'm sure God didn't intend for so many people to be sick. But we have poisoned our food and polluted our air, water and soil until our doctors are dying from overwork. If you want to know my secret, you can read my booklet, *No Aches, No Pains, No Drugs.* At any rate, I'm delighted to tell you unreservedly and unconditionally that when we all get to heaven, there will be no more pain.

Yes, heaven will be a wonderful place because there will be no tears, no crying, no sorrow, no sickness, no pain and no death.

Right now I want to add another one, even though it isn't mentioned in so many words. Yet by putting together all the things the Bible says about heaven, I know this is true.

THERE WILL BE NO MONOTONY IN HEAVEN

Occasionally I meet people who seem just a little bit worried because they are afraid heaven will be boring. They make a mental list of the things they do every day here on earth, and they are afraid that suddenly when they enter heaven, everything will stop. There'll be no meals to prepare, no dishes to wash, no housecleaning to do, no babies to diaper, no office to go to, no cars to take to the garage, no medical appointments, no operations to talk about, no pains to complain about, no hairdresser's appointments, no shopping, no smoking, no drinking, no filthy jokes, no formal studying, no exams, no football games, no resting, no sleeping—so, what in the world will we do?

God has chosen not to reveal too much. He wants it to be a surprise. But He has told us enough that we can say with the song writers: "Heaven Is a Wonderful Place" and "The Half Has Never Yet Been Told."

The Bible does say, "At thy right hand there are pleasures for evermore" (Ps. 16:11). So who wouldn't exchange the things he must do everyday for perpetual pleasures? What are those pleasures?

For one thing: *Music*—divine, heavenly music which we will make ourselves—both vocal and instrumental. We'll thrill with that music and we'll never get tired of it.

For another thing: *Fellowship*—with those we love—all of God's children—hundreds of millions of them. What a lot of pleasure that will give us. Everybody enjoys dear friends even now. In heaven it will be far better.

For another thing: *Exploration*—all over God's heaven. Since we are finite, and considering the nature of God, I think we'll go on learning about God as we explore the wonders of His heaven for all eternity. And, oh, such indescribable beauty!

For another thing: *Pets*—we'll have horses. I have already talked about that in Message No. 7.

Then, too, there will be: *Food*—good news? I'll talk about that later in chapter 21.

And, of course, there will be: *Worship*—of our Lord whom we love with a perfect love. More of this later, too.

Finally, I must repeat that God in His Word has drawn back the veil of eternity only a tiny crack, so to speak. We have only a glimpse. But we know THERE WILL BE NO DISAPPOINTMENTS IN HEAVEN.

That means everything is on the positive side. Whatever it will take to make you deliriously happy—not for a moment, but forever—that will be there. So relax and anticipate the joys that await you. Don't let Satan turn you into a doubting Thomas or a sour saint. But rather pray without ceasing, rejoice everymore, run the race, press toward the mark, don't grow weary in well doing, lift up your head and sing. You are bound for the

Promised Land.

Back to verse 4. One reason why heaven will be a wonderul place will be because "former things are passed away."

SAD MEMORIES OBLITERATED

People wonder: "Can I enjoy heaven if my unsaved mother is not there? If I look around and discover my husband is missing, can I be happy?" Remember, there is no sorrow, and I think that means God will blot out all memories that might produce sadness. How He will do it, we don't know, but we do know there can be absolutely *no* sorrow in heaven. In this life we have great concern for our friends and loved ones, and we should. But when we get to heaven, all that will be over. Remember, it says:

> . . . for the former things are passed away.
>
> And he that sat upon the throne said, Behold, I make all things new. And he said unto me, Write: for these words are true and faithful.
>
> And he said unto me, It is done. I am Alpha and Omega, the beginning and the end. I will give unto him that is athirst of the fountain of the water of life freely.
>
> He that overcometh shall inherit all things; and I will be his God, and he shall be my son (Rev. 21:4-7).

There is God's offer. Are you "thirsty" for such a place, such a body, such experiences? Then God says, "Come and be my son." It is all paid for, and it is yours for the taking.

At this point we pause to consider the fate of all those who reject the invitation of eternal life.

In verse 8 we have a brief picture of

THE ETERNAL STATE OF THE LOST

> But the fearful, and unbelieving, and the abominable, and murderers, and whoremongers, and sorcerers, and idolaters, and all liars, shall have their part in the lake which burneth with fire and brimstone: which is the second death.

Reread that verse carefully and then ponder this thought. These people are in hell because they refused the cleansing power of the blood of Christ to wash away their guilt. They rejected the offer of the free gift of eternal life.

By contrast, observe that the other group, saved and in heaven, is made up of people who at one time committed these same sins. They were fearful like the disciples on the Sea of Galilee; they were unbelieving like Thomas after the resurrection; they were murderers like Moses; they were immoral like David; they were liars like Ananias and Sapphira, but at this point they are in heaven. So what is the difference? Much indeed! Listen to the apostle Paul explain it. ". . . such were some of you: but ye are washed, but ye are sanctified, but ye are justified in the name of the Lord Jesus . . ." (I Cor. 6:11).

The people in heaven are all sinners saved by the blood of Christ. The people in hell are all sinners who rejected the only One who could save them. That's the difference. Acceptance or rejection of Christ. And at this point in time, when eternity has begun, it's too late to make a choice.

Now we are ready for verses 9 and 10:

> And there came unto me one of the seven angels which had the seven vials full of the seven last plagues, and talked with me, saying, Come hither, I will shew thee the bride, the lamb's wife.
> And he carried me away in the spirit to a great and high mountain, and shewed me that great city, the holy Jerusalem, descending out of heaven from God.

Notice, the angel here is recognized by John as one of the seven special angels we've seen again and again throughout this book.

THE HOLY CITY

He offers to show John the bride and then shows him her home—the Holy City. John calls it "that great city, the holy Jerusalem."

Notice, too, it is moving down through space. It is probably approaching the new earth. Some think it comes to rest on the earth. We really don't know, but I'm inclined to think that it does because all the saved of all ages will dwell together with God—not in separate places. I think the new earth will be far bigger than this present planet and far different in every way.

One thing we can say for sure: John ran out of earthly words as he tried to describe the heavenly city.

For a moment, try to see what John saw. There on the one hand, was the new, beautiful, glorified earth, and approaching it, coming down out of the blue, was the holy Jerusalem, prepared as a bride adorned for her husband, sparkling like a diamond in the sun. What a dazzling spectacle—magnificent beyond human description! John refers to precious gems as he describes the radiance of this city.

Verse 11:

Having the glory of God: and her light was like unto a stone most precious, even like a jasper stone, clear as crystal.

TWELVE GATES

Verses 12-15:

And had a wall great and high, and had twelve gates, and at the gates twelve angels, and names written thereon, which are the names of the twelve tribes of the children of Israel:

On the east three gates; on the north three gates; on the south three gates; and on the west three gates.

And the wall of the city had twelve foundations, and in them the names of the twelve apostles of the Lamb.

And he that talked with me had a golden reed to measure the city, and the gates thereof, and the wall thereof.

And verse 21:

And the twelve gates were twelve pearls: every several gate was of one pearl. . . .

Also verse 25:

And the gates of it shall not be shut at all by day: for there shall be no night there.

The city is no jail. It has twelve huge gates which are literally entrances. These gateways are never closed. We will come and go at will, entering or leaving the city, but always in the eternal state called heaven.

Each "gate" is made of an enormous, heavenly pearl beyond our comprehension and, of course, it will be far more beautiful than any pearl ever taken from any oyster.

In the museum of Istanbul, where the treasures of the Sultans are displayed, one can see some fabulous pearls. One throne chair is studded with 25,000 pearls. And, of course, there are very valuable, rare, large individual pearls on display. They are splendid and radiant to our earthly eyes, but in comparison to the huge, heavenly pearls, they are nothing but specks of dirt. Wait till you see those gates that are made of pearl.

THE CITY LIES FOURSQUARE

Verse 16:

> And the city lieth foursquare, and the length is as large as the breadth: and he measured the city with the reed, twelve thousand furlongs. The length and the breadth and the height of it are equal.

CUBE OR PYRAMID?

John says the city has the same dimension every way you measure it. The length, the breadth, and the height of it are all equal. This could mean a cube or it could mean a pyramid; I really don't know which. The Living Bible, which adds its own commentary to the translation, says: "... in fact it was in the form of a cube." But the actual words John used do not say this. It only says that it has the same dimensions each of three ways: length, breadth and height. In other words, it was exactly as long as it was wide as it was high. Now that could be a pyramid. I'm inclined to think it is.

There is something beautiful, fascinating, and mysterious about a pyramid. The occult world often takes its perverted teachings from some remote basis of fact. It just might be possible that the heavenly city is in fact a pyramid. Maybe God told Adam and Adam told Methuselah and so the early inhabitants of earth, including those in the valley of the Nile, held a profound respect for a pyramid. Considering the fact that the pyramids were to be temporary abodes until their contents could be transferred to the next world, this could at least be a possibility. I realize I'm speculating and I hope you won't misquote what I said.

There is another thought I must share with you. The city *lies* foursquare. Does this refer to the base of the city while the superstructure is not square—only equal in height to the sides of the base? It could be.

So much for its shape. Now let's talk about how big the city is.

THE SIZE OF THE CITY

In verse 16 John says it is 12,000 furlongs—which in our figures today would be about 1,500 miles. Did you hear that? FIFTEEN HUNDRED MILES—LONG—WIDE—and HIGH! Wow! What a city!

There is absolutely no city on earth that can compare. New York and Los Angeles may stretch out for 50 or 75 miles, but this city is 1,500 miles each way. If it came to rest on the eastern part of the United States, it would reach from the Atlantic Ocean to the Mississippi River and from the border of Canada to the Gulf of Mexico.

It is so high it would take more than 5,000 Empire State buildings on top of each other to match its height—that's higher than the astronauts fly when they orbit around the earth.

And yet some ignorant critics of the Bible have scoffed at the possibility of a city big enough to hold all the people that are supposed to be there. Let me tell you, there will be lots of room—no crowded city. It will be a spacious city. And that's putting it mildly.

THE WALL OF THE CITY

Verses 17 and 18:

And he measured the wall thereof, an hundred and forty and four cubits, according to the measure of a man, that is, of the angel.

And the building of the wall of it was of jasper: and the city was pure gold, like unto clear glass.

Five times, from verse 12 to verse 18, John mentions the wall. He has a good deal to say about it, but he never mentions its purpose. Most certainly it is not for defense. It is 216 feet high. That is, indeed, a high wall as earthly cities go. But when you think of a city that is 1,500 miles high, 216 feet would just be a decorative "border." And that's exactly what I think it is for. There are no closed entrances so there need not be any wall at all for the purpose that earthly walls serve around earthly cities. But this wall adds to the aesthetic beauty and gives it a finished look.

The walls are made of translucent jasper, "clear as crystal," with twelve layers of jewels serving as foundations. Each layer is named after one of Jesus' disciples just as each pearly gate has the name of one of the twelve tribes of Israel. Thus, these twelve Old Testament patriarchs and twelve New Testament apostles are greatly honored in the celestial realm because of the unique position and service they had on earth. Notice now:

THE FOUNDATION JEWELS

Verses 19-21:

> And the foundations of the wall of the city were garnished with all manner of precious stones. The first foundation was jasper; the second, sapphire; the third, a chalcedony; the fourth, an emerald;
>
> The fifth, sardonyx; the sixth, sardius; the seventh, chrysolyte; the eighth, beryl; the ninth, a topaz; the tenth, a chrysoprasus; the eleventh, a jacinth; the twelfth, an amethyst.
>
> And the twelve gates were twelve pearls: every several gate was of one pearl: and the street of the city was pure gold, as it were transparent glass.

The last part of verses 18 and 21 tell us the city itself, including the streets, was made of pure gold. But this heavenly gold is unlike earthly gold; it is transparent. All of this is so far beyond our earthly experience, we cannot grasp the total beauty and splendor of the city whose maker and builder is God.

But stop and meditate on this fact: We are going there! And it won't be long!

Now let's read the rest of chapter 21.

Verses 22-27:

> And I saw no temple therein: for the Lord God Almighty and the Lamb are the temple of it.
>
> And the city had no need of the sun, neither of the moon, to shine in it: for the glory of God did lighten it, and the Lamb is the light thereof.
>
> And the nations of them which are saved shall walk in the light of it: and the kings of the earth do bring their glory and honour into it.
>
> And the gates of it shall not be shut at all by day: for there shall be no night there.
>
> And they shall bring the glory and honour of the nations into it.

And there shall in no wise enter into it any thing that defileth, neither whatsoever worketh abomination, or maketh a lie: but they which are written in the Lamb's book of life.

NO TEMPLE, NO SUN, NO MOON, NO NIGHT AND NO SIN

There are more things that will not be there. These, except for the last one, serve a real purpose here on earth, but in heaven they are not needed because of the very nature of God and the characteristics of our heavenly home.

The Lord who is the source and essence of all light, will, with the brilliance of His own person, radiate total light all over His vast heaven. Is that hard to understand? Yes, it is. But remember, He who made our sun and a hundred billion more suns throughout each of ten billion galaxies can certainly light up heaven. Just wait; you'll see!

HEAVENLY KINGS

And into this heavenly realm the millennial kings will have their honored positions transferred. Remember in chapter 5, the saints in heaven sang about being kings and reigning on the earth. In chapter 19 they came from heaven to reign with the newly crowned King of kings. In chapter 20 they reigned with Him. Now the thousand-year reign has ended, but they will not lose their position and honor as kings (see also Rev. 22:5). All of this is transferred to the eternal state—even though there is no longer any need to "reign" in a practical sense. You'll see why as we explain verse 27.

SIN IS FOREVER ABOLISHED

At this point there can be no sin in heaven. It will be impossible because all redeemed mortals and all the holy angels have been confirmed in righteousness. All beings of all time have made their decisions determining their relation to God and their eternal abode. Therefore, God now abolishes sin as He seals and settles this relationship forever.

Under no condition can there ever be another Lucifer starting a rebellion in heaven. Under no conditions can anyone ever commit sin in heaven. Likewise, the unrighteous, lost souls in hell, according to chapter 22, verse 11, will be confirmed to their lost, sinful estate for an endless eternity.

We come now to the final chapter of the Bible. Whatever God has not yet revealed or whatever He wants to repeat for emphasis, He will do it now. There is only one Bible; there will never be another and this is the last chapter—divided by men into 22 verses for our convenience.

THE GARDEN OF GOD

Verses 1 and 2:

> And he shewed me a pure river of water of life, clear as crystal, proceeding out of the throne of God and of the Lamb.
>
> In the midst of the street of it, and on either side of the river, was there the tree of life, which bare twelve manner of fruit every month: and the leaves of the tree were for the healing of the nations.

Notice, there is a river and there are fruit trees. The tree of life, originally in the Garden of Eden, is now here in the Garden of God. Oh, yes, this is the heart of the city, but it is a garden. Man started in a garden; he will end in a garden-city.

Some of you felt a little sad at the beginning of chapter 21 when John revealed that the oceans of the world were destroyed when the world went up in flame. You'll feel better now to hear that there will be the most beautiful heavenly river you ever saw—clear as crystal, flowing right out of the throne of heaven. In chapter 4, verse 6, John mentions a "sea of glass, like unto crystal" before the throne. I like that. I like water, and I'm glad for what John tells us about water in heaven.

Now I have a feeling some of you want to take your fishing rod along to heaven. Your motor boat and water skis? Your bathing suit? Forget it! These are earthly pleasures God has arranged for us here below. But in heaven we'll advance to another dimension. So rejoice; it will be much better. You'll not lose anything; you'll only gain.

Picture this in your mind and make a sketch of it to help you visualize it better. The main street of heaven (made of pure gold) leads right up to the throne. Coming out from the throne is a river of crystal clear water. (Note: no dirt, no mud, no pollution here!) It flows right down the center of the street.

John says on each side of the river and yet in the center of the street, fruit trees are growing. Not cherry, peach, apple, apricot, plum or pear—no, those are earth trees. We must try to think like a resident of heaven. John says it's the tree of life, and that it bears a variety of fruit every month. "Every month" is earth time. There is no such thing in heaven. So what the Holy Spirit is here revealing is that these trees bear perpetually. We would call them ever-bearing.

WE WILL EAT IN HEAVEN

I'm very fond of fruit and I'm so glad that we'll eat fruit in heaven. Just the fact that we will eat in heaven makes some of you cheer up. Why will we eat? Not to sustain life like we do now. Remember, our heavenly bodies are not energized by blood. Of our earthly bodies, the Bible tells us, the life is in the blood (Lev. 17:11). But our heavenly bodies will be energized by pure spirit and we will not need food to sustain our energy. So why will we eat? Get ready for good news: we will eat for sheer pleasure. Some of you do that already, but with detrimental effects. There will be no such problems in heaven, because there will be no problems at all in heaven. Heaven is a perfect place for perfect people.

I DON'T KNOW

Look at the last sentence of verse 2. After studying this book for 30 years, I must confess I do not know what it means. I praise God that over the years He has let me "see" an ever-increasing number of insights and understandings of otherwise difficult passages. One by one they have unfolded in response to long hours of study, meditation and prayer. But this is one of the few passages in the Bible that as of now I can't explain.

I could spiritualize it, but I see no reason for doing so and I would have no peace of mind about such an explanation. But I do know what it does not mean. It certainly does not mean that our heavenly bodies will get sick.

The Living Bible says, ". . . the leaves were used for the medicine to heal the nations." I think that is ridiculous. Do you think the angels ever take medicine? Not in a million years! And neither will we! I expect that one day God will give me the correct explanation. Until He does, I will eagerly await the pleasure of eating the most delicious heavenly fruit one could ever dream of.

THE CURSE WILL BE COMPLETELY GONE

Verse 3:

> And there shall be no more curse: but the throne of God and of the Lamb shall be in it; and his servants shall serve him.

When sin entered the human race, God was forced to reduce paradise to a place of problems and difficulties. God introduced thorns, thistles, weeds, pests, pain and work—all to remind man that he is a sinner and needs a savior. The earth itself doesn't like it. This planet is groaning to be relieved of the curse (Rom. 8:22).

Now, while sin is rampant, the curse is heavy. During the kingdom age, when there will be much less sin, the curse will be light. In the eternal state, where there will be no sin, the curse will be gone.

It is interesting to observe how man, with all his scientific know-how, is constantly trying to erase the curse himself—apart from God. When I was a boy they told us that by the time we were grown-up, everything would be so wonderful that living on earth would be living in a paradise. Radios, television, automatic washers, dryers, dishwashers, refrigerators, freezers, running hot and cold water, automatic heating and cooling, electric gadgets of every kind, tractors, harvesters, balers, shellers, feeders, stable cleaners, automobiles, airplanes—all these and more would usher in utopia.

So here we are, fifty years later, and what is the picture? Oh, we have all of these things all right, just like they said. But they didn't mention: riots, robberies, murders, pollution, pesticide poisonings, cancer, heart failures, arthritis, sleeping pills and harmful drugs—to say nothing of famine, earthquakes, tornadoes, death rays and atomic bombs.

All these and many more are threatening to wipe out the human race before the next fifty years go by. Of course, that will never happen. The record we have in Revelation enables us to say that man will never destroy himself because God will intervene. We know how it's all coming out. So cheer up, we are going to heaven where there will be NO MORE CURSE.

WE SHALL SERVE HIM

Notice the last sentence of verse 3: ". . . and his servants shall serve him." I don't know all that statement involves, but I know it will be pure pleasure. Remember, He loved us so much He died for us so that we could enjoy all the bliss of heaven. At this point we will love with a divine love beyond anything our earthly hearts can feel. Not only that, but look at verse 4.

And they shall see his face; and his name shall be in their foreheads.

WE SHALL ADORE HIM

If you look with a prolonged gaze at a beautiful earth person, it is called "staring." But when we get to heaven, we shall spend a great deal of time just looking at the most beautiful sight in all of the eternal state—His face. We will enjoy it, and so will He. It is called adoration and worship. You can add this to the list of activities that will keep us busy in heaven.

FINAL SUMMARY AND CONCLUSION — Verses 5-21

Now read carefully verses 5 and 6.

And there shall be no night there; and they need no candle, neither light of the sun; for the Lord God giveth them light: and they shall reign for ever and ever.

And he said unto me, These sayings are faithful and true: and the Lord God of the holy prophets sent his angel to shew unto his servants the things which must shortly be done.

There are 17 verses left and God's revelation will be finished.

The sacred canon will then be complete. God will never give any additional written information to man. The Bible will be finished.

This is a summary in which God repeats for the sake of emphasis some things He told us before.

GOD'S PURPOSE FOR THIS BOOK

God's purpose for this book is to reveal to His children what the future holds for them. Knowing that your future happiness is assured, you should rejoice now, even in the midst of suffering and sorrow, because all these things are only for a little while. After that, there will be only perpetual peace and pleasure.

If you were God and had only a few more sentences to tell men whatever else needed to be said, what do you think you'd say. Notice how God handles it.

THE AUTHORITY OF THIS BOOK

In verse 6, He says this record is accurate and correct. Having studied how we got our Bible, and how God miraculously preserved it for nearly 2,000 years against all it's vicious enemies, I am satisfied that we have the essential Word of God in our Bible today. He also says that He is the God of the Bible prophets, so we can trust their prophecies. And I have found that to be true.

In verse 8 we have the eyewitness' testimony "I John *saw* . . . and *heard*. . . ."

In verse 13 the divine author says, "I am Alpha and Omega." And in verse 16, He identifies Himself by name: "I Jesus . . . am the root and offspring of David. . . ." That's clear and that's final. You can trust the authenticity of this book.

Now verses 7 through 16:

Behold, I come quickly: blessed is he that keepth the sayings of the prophecy of this book.

And I John saw these things, and heard them. And when I had heard and seen, I fell down to worship before the feet of the angel which shewed me these things.

Then said he unto me, See thou do it not: for I am thy fellow-servant, and of thy brethren the prophets, and of them which keep the sayings of this book: worship God.

And he saith unto me, Seal not the sayings of the prophecy of this book: for the time is at hand.

He that is unjust, let him be unjust still: and he which is filthy, let him be filthy still: and he that is righteous, let him be righteous still: and he that is holy, let him be holy still.

And, behold, I come quickly; and my reward is with me, to give every man according as his work shall be.

I am Alpha and Omega, the beginning and the end, the first and the last.

Blessed are they that do his commandments, that they may have right to the tree of life, and may enter in through the gates into the city.

For without are dogs, and sorcerers, and whoremongers, and murderers, and idolaters, and whatsoever loveth and maketh a lie.

I, Jesus have sent mine angel to testify unto you these things in the churches. I am the root and the offspring of David, and the bright and morning star.

THE PROMISE OF HIS COMING

It is significant that Christ mentions three times in these final verses that He is coming suddenly without warning. "Behold" means "attention, this is important." So in verse 7 He says "Behold, I come quickly." In verse 12 He repeats exactly the same thing, and we'll see it again in verse 20. Thus, Christ emphasizes His return more than any other one thing in the summary of His final revelation to man. How important then, this must be!

GOD'S FINAL INSTRUCTION
TO WORSHIP AND WITNESS

The last two words of verse 9 are a repetition of chapter 19, verse 10: Worship God. This must be important. In verse 10 we are told to open this book. That surely is for the purpose of *reading* it. In verse 16 Jesus says His messenger (angel) shall testify or proclaim these things *in the churches.* The word angel is the word messenger, and I think means preacher in this context. Compare this with verse 11 in chapter 1 where Jesus said this book should be sent to the churches.

Now compare the last sentence of verse 10 of chapter 22 with chapter 1, verse 3. The time is at hand. At the end of Daniel's prophecy, God told Daniel, ". . . the words are closed up and sealed till the time of the end" (Dan. 12:9).

More than 600 years later God told John ". . . Seal not . . . this book: for the time is at hand." All of this simply means open the book, read it, preach it in the churches, and tell everybody what God has written. Isn't it strange that most churches today keep this book closed.

LAST MENTION OF REWARDS

The last part of verse 12 is a reminder that there will be rewards for the faithful. Paul says this will happen at the Judgment Seat of Christ where we Christians must all appear to give an account of our service to Him. Heaven is a free gift, but good works will merit rewards. Jesus mentions this here among the final important reminders which He doesn't want us to forget.

LAST WARNING ABOUT HELL

In verse 15 we have one last reminder for those who refuse to accept Jesus as Saviour. In their sinful estate they will be condemned to be "out" of the celestial realm, outside the eternal state. Of course, we have already learned that there is only one other place, namely, hell.

A little girl came to me one time after I had preached this sermon. She was worried. "Will all dogs end up in hell?" she asked with great concern. I was glad to tell her that earthly pets, including dogs, do not live after death. God has given us earthly pets to enjoy in this life; I think it's very likely we'll have much more wonderful heavenly pets to enjoy in the next world.

But the word dogs is here used to speak of that which is low, despicable, and dirty. The Jews used this word to indicate what they thought of the Samaritans. So the word "dogs" is used in verse 15 in speaking of unregenerate sinners who will be eternally separated from God—out of His presence forever.

LAST INVITATION TO HEAVEN

Verse 17:

> And the Spirit and the bride say, Come. And let him that heareth say, Come. And let him that is athirst, come. And whosoever will, let him take the water of life freely.

This invitation comes from the Holy Spirit and from the church which is this bride. Anyone who hears and accepts is then instructed to join those who are giving the invitation. So every newborn babe in Christ should be a soul winner, telling others the good news and inviting them to come along to heaven. WHOSOEVER WILL—COME ON!

LAST WARNING: DON'T CHANGE THE BOOK

Verses 18 and 19:

> For I testify unto every man that heareth the words of the prophecy of this book, If any man shall add unto these things, God shall add unto him the plagues that are written in this book:
>
> And if any man shall take away from the words of the book of this prophecy, God shall take away his part out of the book of life, and out of the holy city, and from the things which are written in this book.

This is serious. The penalty is the greatest. God warns man not to tamper with His written Word—the Bible. The devil is always doing this, but God's warning is awful. Don't add and don't subtract. In Timothy we are instructed to study so we can rightly divide the Word. That means we should study it so much that we can explain it as one harmonious whole—not explaining it in such a way as to make God contradict Himself. People say you can make the Bible say anything you want to. That is not true when you handle it right.

THE LAST PROMISE IN THE BIBLE

Verse 20:

> He which testifieth these things saith, Surely I come quickly. Amen, Even so, come, Lord Jesus.

It is significant that Christ chose the promise of His return as the last written promise to leave with His children. In verses 7 and 12, as I already pointed out, He says, "Behold, I come quickly." Now for the final statement, He says, "*Surely,* I come quickly." Thus, He emphasizes the certainty of His return. How can it be that so many church-goers have not grasped the reality of the imminent return of Christ?

Jesus *is* coming again! It will surely happen. It will be in person and it will be without warning—like a thief in the night—unannounced. But it will not be unforetold. It is the last promise in the Bible. Are you ready? If He should come today, where would you be tomorrow?

If you love Him who first loved us, then you can pray with John:

THE LAST PRAYER IN THE BIBLE
Even so, come, Lord Jesus

Dr. Louis Bauman was one of the great Bible prophecy preachers of the first half of this century. He went to heaven before I had an opportunity to meet him. But I have read his books. His late widow attended my church for some time, and his son, Dr. Paul Bauman, has been a close friend of mine for 30 years. So I feel I know Dr. Bauman even though we never met. He had a great deal to do with the establishment of Grace Theological Seminary. Ever since I have been a traveling evangelist, I have been meeting people who tell me they were saved under his ministry. He had hoped so much to see the Lord return in his lifetime.

I recall all this to tell you how thrilled I was several years ago when I stood by the grave of this great man of God in the cemetery of the First Brethren Church in America (Germantown, Pennsylvania), and there on his tombstone I read these words: "Even so, come, Lord Jesus."

THE LAST VERSE IN THE BIBLE

Verse 21:

The grace of our Lord Jesus Christ be with you all. Amen.

This is the last verse of God's written revelation to men—the last written message from heaven. So what does God do but pronounce the benediction. It is the last benediction in the Bible. There is nothing we can add to that but to bow in humble adoration and worship as we say: Amen! and Amen! That means: So be it Lord!

LET US PRAY

O God, our Heavenly Father, we stand in awe and reverence before Thee as we think of the fact that the eternal, omnipotent God inspired, guided and guarded the writings of men until they were all written in a book.

We thank Thee for preserving this book for us today. We pray for those in totalitarian countries to whom this book—Your Word—is not available.

Now Lord, we pray if there is anyone here who has not yet believed this record, cause that person to be so convinced by the Holy Spirit that he can hold out no longer. Now that he knows the whole future history of the world, grant that he may make the right decision and surrender his heart and life to the One who alone can save from sin and eternal doom.

Lord, save any who need the Saviour and strengthen every believer in the faith. And, Lord, if we should never meet again on this earth, grant that none shall be missing at that glad reunion in the sky.

In the name of Jesus, Saviour, Lord and coming King, we pray. Amen.

A Personal Letter to All My Rich Readers

Dear Reader,

You are fabulously wealthy. You own a little piece of eternity called NOW. It costs you nothing, and you cannot keep it. But at the last judgment, if it were possible, you could sell this present moment for a million-billion dollars. Every lost soul in hell (when that time comes) would buy it if he could. But then it will be *too late*. Decisions that determine one's eternal destiny must be made on this side of the "great divide" in the *now*.

You have heard what God has to say. Now it's your time to tell Him what you think of Him. In great love, He has offered you a contract involving your reservation for your eternal destiny.

According to the Bible, there are two choices, and only two. These you cannot change. If you have not already done so, you must now make your choice. God demands a verdict. Remember, He loves you and He wants you to love Him but, since love is by choice—not by force—He is giving you the liberty of free choice. Remember, too, to delay or deny the point of decision is the same as keeping your present reservation—and that would be the greatest mistake of your life.

So please check the reservation of your choice and sign it, so it may be read at your funeral. I pray that, for your sake, for the sake of your friends and loved ones, and for the sake of the Lord who died for you, you'll make the right choice.

RESERVATION FOR HELL

Being of sound mind, and by my own free choice, I do hereby declare and proclaim to all who may be concerned, that my choice for my eternal destiny is HELL—the lake of fire.

Date_____ Signed_____

RESERVATION FOR HEAVEN

Being of sound mind and by my own free choice, I do hereby proclaim to all who may be concerned that my choice for my eternal destiny is HEAVEN.

I hereby accept God's written offer to give me eternal life on His terms. Therefore, I pray:

Dear God, I'm a sinner. I want to be saved, but I know I cannot save myself. But I believe that Jesus died for me, and that He can save me. So, dear Jesus, I am, here and now, honestly and sincerely as best I know how, asking You to forgive my sin and give me the gift of eternal life. Come into my heart and save me now.

I hereby accept and receive You as my own personal Saviour and Lord according to Your offer in the Bible. Fill me with Your Spirit. Make me one of Your children. Help me grow spiritually and be more like You each day. I want You to be Lord of my life. Give me inner peace and assurance. Help me to love, trust and obey You in the power of the Holy Spirit. Amen!

Date_____ Signed_____

NOTE: God bless you for your decision. I'd be so glad to hear about it. One soul, you know, is worth more than the whole world.

Will you please drop me a card telling me the date you signed your reservation? I'll thank God and pray for you. I will also send you some free literature that you should find helpful. Include a self-addressed, stamped envelope if you can. Write to me at this address:

> The Nathan Meyer
> Bible Prophecy Association
> P. O. Box 4̶0̶3̶ 442
> Worthington, Ohio 43085